P. Godath.
March 07, 1989
(P. A. INDRAJITH.)

HOW TO GET RICH WHILE YOU SLEEP

NEW REVISED EDITION

by

J. DAVID HUSKIN

and

WILLIAM E. MONSEES

CORNERSTONE LIBRARY
Published by Simon & Schuster, New York

Published by Cornerstone Library, Inc.
A Simon & Schuster Division of
Gulf & Western Corporation
Simon & Schuster Building
1230 Avenue of the Americas
New York, New York 10020

CORNERSTONE LIBRARY and colophon are trademarks of Simon & Schuster,
registered in the U.S. Patent and Trademark Office.

Manufactured in the United States of America
10 9 8 7 6 5 4 3 2 1

ISBN 0-346-12449-2

**To the true professionals of
Real Estate, the CCIM's**

CONTENTS

INTRODUCTION

If you have had much contact with real estate circles in the past twenty years, you've probably heard of Dave Huskin and Bill Monsees. Dave has an investment real estate firm in Denver, but spends most of his time managing his own investments and counselling those who are fortunate enough to be able to afford him. Bill is well known for being one of the country's early real estate educators and has taught people how to invest from coast to coast.

Most of this book was written in 1969, but has been updated and revised several times. Anyone who ten years ago took seriously the advice found in these pages should now be jumping for joy. They are most likely wealthy! The principles and teachings found here are more appropriate now than ever.

Time has proven that these two men know what they are talking about. They wrote this book for those people who do not understand the investment aspects of real estate.

The approach is simple. Huskin and Monsees look at all forms of investing, and they compare each to each other in terms of risk, yield, growth, management, liquidity, predictability and tax shelter. Magic is reduced to common sense.

The book is likely to be controversial. For example, these two guys have socked insurance and savings accounts, and that's sort of like being against motherhood and the Boy Scouts. Of course, they aren't, but they step right up and say what they feel about some of the things that have been said about insurance and savings accounts as forms of investments. Insurance men and bankers aren't going to like it much. But the people who have their money "invested" in each or either are going to be able to give their investment dollars more consideration and thought than ever before.

Whoever you are, banker, lawyer, housewife, insurance peddler, lover, accountant, singer or swinger, you're going to have to agree on one thing after you've read this book. Real estate is one fabulous way to get rich while you sleep.

CHAPTER 1

HOW TO GET RICH WHILE YOU SLEEP

Right after a thing called a day was created, God subdivided it into two parts. And rather than leave it as simple as night and day, someone else sold us on slicing it into three phases—work, play and sleep.

Perhaps it was a philosophical physician who prescribed the parting, but his proposed plan promoted a paved path to a pleasant, productive and prolonged life. With Wednesday afternoons off for golf, it isn't a bad idea to balance life with equal shares of work, play and sleep. But it isn't always possible to live that perfectly.

The work period is designed to force us to produce enough income to provide us with money for play and a place to sleep. The play period gives us time to unwind from the pressures of work, and its specific purpose is to drive us mad with boredom. And this lures us into having fun by spending all of the money we earn at work. Most of us regard these two periods as the productive phases of life. Sleep isn't considered to be a productive activity.

We tend to ignore or hide the fact that we sleep at all. We want to work long enough to earn enough money to go out and play. When the money is gone, we can always go back to work and earn enough money to get back to play. Working and playing hard are admirable traits. But does anyone work or play hard for the reward of sleep? If it were really popular, would we leave it to the last thing we do each day? Sleep seems to be something to do when there's nothing else to do.

Remember that last sales meeting in Denver? You left Cincinnati at seven in the morning. It was five in Denver. You arrived in Denver at a little after half-past nine. It was eleven-thirty in Cincinnati. You were ready for lunch, and the Denver guys announced a coffee break. By high noon your appetite had lost its edge, and you were ready for the afternoon coffee break. When the afternoon coffee break came, you were ready to belt a few at cocktail time. And when cocktail time came, you were the guy who ate all of the hors d'oeuvres.

You yawned through dinner, but managed to cram the twelve-dollar steak down because all the other guys were having a good time. And after dinner, after all of you had seen the shows at five swell places, you noticed that you were getting your second wind. But the other guys were beginning to fade.

"C'mon," they said, "it's late. Let's get some sleep."

"Sleep?" you said, "it's almost time to get up in Cincinnati."

But because they threatened to abandon you, you agreed to go back to the hotel. By two-thirty you were in bed. It was four-thirty in Cincinnati, and you'd been up for twenty-three hours. Who said sleep was as important as work or play?

At six the hotel operator called and announced in a bright tone that it was six o'clock and a bright, sunny morning. You made the meeting at nine, the coffee break at nine-thirty, lunch at noon, coffee at two-thirty, cocktails at the airport at six. You said good-bye to the boss when you got on the plane at seven, and you settled back for a nap at a quarter to eight. At eight the stewardess shook you, took your order for two bottles of gin, and cracked your knee with the tray on the back of the seat in front of you. You ate a well-done, steamed steak over St. Louis, and she took your tray just as the wheels went down for the landing at Cincinnati.

Your wife met you, and she looked swell in her new suit. "There's a new group at the Gibson Hotel. Want to go for a drink?" she asked. You went to the Gibson. You had a couple of drinks and you danced on the small floor. She had a ball. You made it home at three and set the alarm for six. When you finally shut the light out, you tried to figure just how much work, play and sleep you had had in the past two days. You lost count, but you figured you had too much work, little play and no sleep at all.

The point of the story is this: You managed to combine work and a little play on the trip. But what about the sleep? There wasn't much of it, agreed. But when you were sleeping you weren't able to play or work. Nearly everyone has the ability to combine work and play, but very few know how to get anything but rest out of sleep.

Sleep seems to be the bastard in life. It robs us of time we could spend, want to spend, working or playing. Is sleep a waste of time? If we could find a better way to rest, probably we would. Since we can't, why not find something to produce for us while we are sleeping?

Sleep might be a waste of time. But, if it is, it doesn't have to be a waste of money. There is a way to get rich while sleeping. A small percentage of Americans take advantage of it. And you'd never dream . . . so to speak . . . just how easy and uninvolved it is to get rich while you're asleep.

It is a method of letting something else work for you all the time, even when you are asleep. It involves almost no work at all on your part. It involves being able to make money, which is fun, and it is one of the few possible methods of combining sleep and play. And that's a mad combination to consider.

That's what this book is all about. It's a *how to* book. More than that, it is a *how to know how to* book. We intend to show proof of the method, through success stories, that you can either dream about or do something about. We'll show you that the difference between the haves and have-nots boils down to the dids and the did-nots. Which are you?

CHAPTER 2

THE OTHER 5 PER CENT

There are lots of ways to let money make money for you. For example, we've all been taught to save our money in safe places like banks, savings and loan associations and credit unions. We like the feeling we get when we can hold the little bank book which records our marvelous progress. We like the fact that our money earns interest just because we're willing to let the safe place hold it for us.

But you'll see in this book that a savings account can be a big waste of money. We know this will run against the smooth grain of the bankers, but we can't help ourselves about that. We intend to present facts about investing, and we don't think a savings account is a very good investment.

And as long as we're taking a shot or two at the banking business, we might just as well get a thing or two off our chests about insurance companies. Many, many people feel that insurance is a fine investment. But it isn't. Let's explore these two areas for a little while.

All of us grow up with the idea that we have to save our money. We learn this from our fathers, who learned it from their fathers. Having a savings account in America is part of the customary life we lead. And we agree that everyone should have a certain amount in a savings account to cover family emergencies. But it is silly to have too much more than that in savings.

We've been told, however, that a savings account will provide all of the things we need when we reach an age of retirement. Ads and dads pound it into us constantly. Save for a vacation. Save for your child's college education. Save for retirement. Save. Save. Save.

Convinced, we join things like the payroll savings plan or the Christmas Club, and we dump a little each month or so into the account. The banks offer us interest for keeping the money in their hands, and the savings and loan associations offer a little more.

So much accumulates that we can't expect them to have room for all of it, and we're understanding when they loan our money to other people. Even we can borrow from the bank or the savings and loan. We know the money is protected, or guaranteed, and we do not have to worry about it at all. It is safe.

Insurance companies are a little different. Policies are paid regularly. Millions and millions of dollars pour into the insurance company accounts each month. We don't really know what they do with it, but we know that if we die our heirs will be taken care of. And, of course, there are the policies which mature at a certain rate of interest in a certain length of time. To many, insurance is a good, solid, profitable investment. But we don't think it is.

The primary thing banks and insurance companies do with our money is to invest it in American industry and real estate. By using other people's money, the owners of these institutions prosper on earnings of 6 to 25 per cent while paying out an average of only 3 to 10½ per cent for the use of the money. That's a good return . . . for them. And if you want to really have the possibility of getting rich while sleeping, start a bank or an insurance company.

When we're in school we learn all about diagramming sentences, how to multiply x times y to get z, how to bake a pie, how to speak and read a foreign language and how to write a letter. But no one teaches us about investing. With the exception of what we may have been given in college courses, none of us has the needed exposure in how to take care of the money we might earn in the next forty or fifty years. So we learn about it from our fathers, who learned from their fathers, who probably didn't know any more about it than most of us did when we were in the eighth grade.

One of the reasons we have to take pot shots at some strictly American customs, such as banking, insurance and education, is that we have proof that what they do might be fine for many, but it doesn't really help anyone, out of the mass of people who struggle through life, to end up as financial successes when they reach sixty-five. Did you know that 95 per cent of the people in this country over the age of sixty-five today are financial failures? Well, it's true. Only 5 per cent of the people over sixty-five today are in the class of success.

That seems a little sad. We live in the richest nation in the history of the world. Opportunity is here. We have massive talent. We can step on the moon, and we can muster up enough money to buy anything we need. But 95 per cent of us are financial failures at the age of sixty-five.

We didn't make up the figures. They came from a survey conducted by the United States Government. The primary purpose of the survey was to study the people living in America who might be eligible for the Medicare Plan. But the findings revealed much more than that.

The survey showed, first of all, that there were 19 million people in the United States over the age of sixty-five. It showed that 95 per cent of these 19 million can be classified as nonwealthy. And that means, simply, that 95 per cent of these people are either still working because they have to work, or depend on social security, charity or their children for their existence. It's sad to think that 95 out of 100 people can wind up broke when they reach the age of retirement.

Assuming that we begin our working days at an average age of twenty, we have about forty-five productive years to either succeed or fail financially. Those of us who make it through high school earn about $767,000 during that time. College graduates will earn upwards of $1,027,000. That's a whole sackful of money, and it's sad to think that nearly all of us have the ability to do almost nothing with it during our earning years.

The survey included everyone over the age of sixty-five. This means doctors, lawyers, fire chiefs, butchers, bakers and basket makers. It included men and women, and it included those who had always been rich and those who had always been poor. It was a complete cross section of America's Senior Set. How could they wind up broke?

Most of them learned from their fathers that it was important to save one's money, and the best place to do that was in banks, savings and loan associations, credit unions, etc. And the majority of them saved their money in cash value life insurance, which happens to be one of the largest single sources of cash savings for the American people.

They saved in these safe places because their money was *guaranteed*. These institutions guarantee to protect the principal and to pay interest. But, as we said, they don't just stuff it in the vault and forget it until you want it back. They invest it in American industry and real estate.

The success of these businesses is based on a simple formula. They use the money given to them by savers or investors or policy holders, and they invest it at a higher rate than they pay. Sure they can guarantee the money. And, also, they can guarantee not to pay us more interest than the specified rate . . . regardless of what they earn through their own shrewd investing. They use other people's money (ours) and they grow rich while 95 per cent of us go broke.

Insurance companies employ some of the best salesmen in the world. Everyone has some kind of insurance, and many, many people still feel that insurance is a good investment. But what about that 95 per cent who failed? They were sold on the packages of financial security offered by the insurance companies. And where did it get them? Nowhere. In trouble. Is that progress or security? Hell, no, it isn't. It's failure.

What about the other 5 per cent? What about those who made it? What did they do that was so radically different from the rest?

These people, the ones in the other 5 per cent, were considered financially independent by the survey. It doesn't mean they are rich, but they are able to support themselves without working, and none of them depend on children or other charities for existence. How did they do it? They bypassed the guarantee, and they invested directly in American industry and real estate. That's right, they did the same thing the banks and the insurance companies do.

While we have to stomp on some powerful toes in this book, our purpose is not to dust fingers at the poor 95 per cent of the people over sixty-five. We're more interested in looking into why the other 5 per cent succeeded. Who knows, we might be sixty-five one of these days, and we want to make darn sure we're qualified for the right club.

We're not afraid to tell on banks and insurance companies because we're telling the story like it is. If you're going to get any good out of what we have to say, then you are going to have to put aside many of the well-established ideas of prudence, investing and earning. By doing this you'll see many of the financial "big brothers" as they really are.

And we don't want you to think for a moment that we don't have some insurance or that we keep our money in a tin can under the loose step on the back porch. We think insurance and banks are important, but we don't think of either of them as investments.

We intend to show you what you must learn about money and how to put it to work for you. And we plan to show the American financial scene as it is. It is full of deception and it is not understood by many, but it offers tremendous opportunity.

We will try to tell you the financial story from all sides. After you've read the book, of course, you'll have to decide what to do with your own investments. You might decide on real estate, you might decide on the stock market, you might decide on savings, and you might decide on insurance. But remember this: 95 per cent of the people in the United States blew it. Only 5 per cent made it. And financial success isn't that mysterious. Money is just a tool.

CHAPTER 3

UNDERSTANDING MONEY

Money is a medium of exchange. It is a measure of value. It may be used as payment for goods or services. Money is an investor and a capitalist tool. It is used to accomplish financial goals. And since it takes goods, men, machines and money to produce goods or services, we must have a thorough understanding of all of these because they are economic factors. We learn what men and machines and goodies are when we are very young, but some of us never learn to understand money.

People forget, or never learn, that there can't be any produce without money, or capital. And capital is the money invested to make the produce. All productions require capital. The *rent* on this capital can be based on an equity or a fixed return. But the capital is only attracted when a prospect of earning the *rent* and preserving the capital exists.

Remember this and you'll prevent the economic hardships experienced with the unfortunate 95 per cent. When money is invested very wisely it helps us reach our goals. On the other hand, money invested unwisely is erosion to the tool we need most, and that's money. This doesn't mean that you have to be a sour Scrooge with your money. It means you have to be careful with it, but you have to use it. After all, money is the basic tool to make life easier for us, not more difficult.

Have you thought about how it would be if we didn't have a form of money or currency? Without it, specialization would be impossible. We would have to operate on a barter economy, maybe trading a bean for an olive and a glass of bourbon for a glass of gin. That's a tough way to get a martini. It's a whole lot easier to buy one at the saloon for a thing called a dollar.

But the greatest economy known to mankind has existed in the United States. The abundance is due to our financial and political climate, which is conducive to attracting capital. In turn, this capital has provided the machines, paid the manpower and provided the know-how to remove the overburden covering production. More production led to more jobs, and the men doing the work spent most of their money, but they managed to save some of it, and became capitalists. It's a cycle. The only time the cycle is interrupted is when our government takes unfavorable action to disturb progress.

But money is the tool necessary in our economic cycle. We have to know how to use this tool, and we have to know how to take care of it. We have to protect it from theft, loss, erosion or excessive harsh use, which might be called excessive or high risk. And when we apply our knowledge to the investment dollar, it's easy to see how we must use and protect these special funds.

We feel that no one can hope to become even partially financially independent without wise investing. In a book called *The Rich and The Super Rich,* the author, Professor Ferdinand Lundberg, states:

"... Anyone who does not own a fairly substantial amount of income-producing property or does not receive an earned income sufficiently large to make substantial regular savings or does not hold a well-paid securely tenured job is poor."

That's his definition of poverty. We agree with part of what the good professor says. We think he's right on target about the owning of income-producing property, and we agree that the lack of it can lead to poverty. However, in a typically academic way, he fails to realize that there cannot be such a thing as a "tenured job" because if you can't produce, the pay ultimately ends. Furthermore, Professor Lundberg is naive in believing that savings can be wrought from ordinary income in sufficient amounts to make the saver financially successful. Sorry, Professor, but we can prove that savings in non-equity investments have been one of the greatest causes of poverty. We feel that savings are important and necessary, but we think their value lies in accumulating enough capital to purchase an equity investment.

Of course, you must keep your money where it will be safe. But few people understand where money is safe. American people have invested in life insurance cash reserves to the stinging tune of $159 billion. The money is being eroded by inflation, and the small money earner has been bamboozled by slick salesmen from the insurance companies. He has fallen for their propaganda, and he believes they will be providing for happy futures in a riskless way by putting his money into ordinary life insurance or other low-yield, fixed-return, inflation-deteriorating investments. Of course, even some insurance salesmen believe their own story. Sad, but true. They are brainwashed by "Big Brother."

Ignorance is the cause of poverty. Stupidity, lack of education and poor education at all levels have resulted in a general lack of money understanding in America. If you don't know what to do with a dollar, how can you do more than spend it? We are victims of financial ignorance, and the 95 per cent who didn't make it are proof—poor, yet living proof—that most Americans don't know a damn thing about money.

For the most part we are ready to buy almost anything. Just sell us something, and we'll buy it. Current television commercials are examples of just how gullible we are. We don't care so much what it costs, just as long as it'll make us sexy or appear richer and more successful. But if someone tried to sell something like education on television, with all gimmicks taken out, it probably wouldn't sell. The only helpful programs on the air today about real things going on in America are found on the educational television station. The programs aren't strong enough with sex or violence or insane comedy to lure sponsors, and they wind up on the ETV station. And what happens? No one watches because they'd rather see a cowboy kiss his horse or ride off into the sunset.

And even the ETV stations don't have many programs about money. They show what's new and different about Japanese cooking and modern math, but they don't show how you can build two dimes into five dimes. Why don't they do a program on how to get rich? Is it a crime to want to be prosperous?

Why don't the ETV stations show programs on insurance or banking or the stock market or how to invest in real estate? Why don't the public schools teach anything about how to manage one's money? It is the only thing almost everyone in this nation has at one time or another. It is tragic that we don't know more about money. And the results of our stupidity show in the survey about the 95 per cent who goofed.

Public and private schools have weathered many attacks against them for their failure to stay ahead in science and math, but who condemns them for failing to teach our children about money? And we don't propose that knowing about money is more important than knowing about science or math, but we do feel that money ought to have some attention. Have you ever known anyone who could do without it?

Few, if any, grade schools and high schools teach a student the meaning of an investment. No classroom instruction, except in very rare cases, is spent telling a young boy how to manage the money he makes working at the corner drugstore. And girls don't have the slightest idea about supermarket prices or the feeding of soon-to-come families on the money to be given to them by their young husbands.

But they'll buy a television set so they can watch hours and hours of garbage. And while they watch the slop on television, the Madison Avenue boys take over during the commercials. They can con a young couple into buying a new Mustang before they buy an old sofa. They can con young and old alike into buying anything . . . because who needs money? You don't need money. You need credit. With credit you can buy nearly anything you want. Whether you want it or not a credit card may be mailed to you.

So the kids go into hock at the bank. Both of them go to work to make the payments on the Mustang, and by the time they get it paid off, the Mustang is worn out. And there's nothing for them to do but grab hold of the brass ring on the merry-go-round and go in a little deeper for another car.

Who should have told them about all of this? Their parents? What do they know? The schools should have told their parents about money, and the schools should have told the kids about money.

An astounding educational lack does exist when it comes to money . . . the basic thing all of us need. Even business colleges graduate thousands who don't know anything about money. They don't know an investment from a ticket to a football game. And most of them don't know how to do anything with money except to spend it.

Well, we intend to do something about it. We know about money because we are interested in making a success out of life . . . a financial success as well as a personal success. If you're a parent, tell your kids what we have to say in this book about money and investments. And if you're a kid, tell your parents. Don't wind up in that 95 per cent. There isn't any reason for financial failure if you know and understand the basics of money and wise investing.

Remember the meaning of money. It is a medium of exchange, and it is a measure of value. It can be used as payment for goods and services. And it is your basic tool of investment.

THE THEORY OF INVESTMENT

Let's boil down the word *investment*. Dictionaries define it as the *investing* of money or capital to gain interest or income. And, as usual, you can't make any sense out of the definition until you know what they mean when they say *investing*.

Invest means to lay out money (which also means capital) in business with the idea of making a profit. It means to put money to use. And the definition doesn't have anything to do with good or bad investments. An investment just *is*, in the basic sense of the word.

To illustrate this, consider what a hippie friend of ours says about the weather. "Man," he says, "the weather ain't good or bad, it just *is!*" And that's the way with the basic concept of the word *investment*. If you want to invest in something, you'll find out in a little while whether it is a good or a bad investment.

We also asked the hippie friend to define *investment* for us, and he said, "Well, you see, man, you lay a little bread on the line and you hope you end up with a whole loaf."

So, considering both definitions, *investing is what you do when you put money to use.*

Without investments, the average person has little chance to save for his heart's desire. He has little chance of obtaining anything that he cannot purchase from his ordinary income. It's the old work-play-work story. The average person spends everything he earns on living. If he receives a raise in salary, it is eaten up quickly by a rise in the cost of living.

The only way he can get ahead financially is through wise fiscal planning. And wise fiscal planning calls for saving, which means accumulating capital. When he has accumulated enough capital to meet emergencies, he should begin transferring his excess funds into an equity position. In other words, when he has earned and saved enough to carry him through financial emergencies, he will be in a position to invest. He'll be in a position to use his extra money to gain more money. He'll be able to put that extra money to work for him.

We gave the banks a licking earlier in the book, but we want to say something nice about them here. A man has to put his money in the bank. It has to be safe. He has to accumulate a savings. But he doesn't have to let the pile grow to a point of dry rot. We like banks. We just don't like what they tell people about investing all of their money in a savings account.

Saving is absolutely necessary for anyone who wants to do more than live a hand-to-mouth way of life. And once the savings will stand off emergencies, you need to make the capital grow. To do this, the capital must be put to work.

There are four basic ways to accumulate capital. You can marry it, inherit it, steal it or save it.

Of course, there are combinations. For example, you could marry a rich thief who had just inherited a wad. When you look at the four methods, however, saving money is just about the only legal, safe way for most of us to accumulate money. But, who knows? You probably do have a rich uncle somewhere who will leave his estate to you. Until that happens, however, save your money. Learn to put these theories to use. And when the lawyer comes to your house with the happy news that your beloved Uncle Clyde died and left you a million bucks, you'll know what to do with the money after you have shed the proper number of tears. Of course the tax man will be there to help you through your grief, but he'll go away just as soon as you part with some of dear old Clyde's cash.

Under today's tax laws, combined with the high cost of living, it is almost impossible to accumulate capital or savings without investing.

You can only work so many hours a day. If you are salaried, you have to do what you can with what you earn during the work phase of your life. And if you're ever going to get ahead of the game, the financial game, then you must put your money to work. Even if there's just a little extra, put it to work.

Investments are designed to supplement ordinary income from a trade, profession or business. And they should be designed to provide money when you, the earner, cannot provide it. An investment should produce earnings without requiring an important contribution by you of your time.

Okay, that's the theory of investments. You need money, also called capital, to invest. Let's call it capital. That'll make the bankers feel a little better about us. Better yet, let's call it by either name. Money is capital, and capital is money. And money is essential to investments in any economic structure. Money is the measure of wealth, it is the keystone of wealth, to sufficient supply and to progress.

THE BASICS OF INVESTMENT

Before investing money in anything, the investor must know enough about economics to judge the worth of his proposed venture: Is it a good deal, or is it a bad deal? If you have money to invest, you'd better be able to make that decision. If you can't but you still want to invest, then ask someone to help you. Don't go into anything without weighing the economics of what you're thinking about doing. Don't ask a hippie, and don't ask your favorite grade school teacher. If you need advice, ask someone who is qualified to give you an opinion. And then ask him if he has any money invested in the thing you are considering. That'll tell you a great deal. Remember, good advice must come from a knowledgeable and impartial source. When we talk about impartial advice in money matters we speak of someone who was originally impartial enough to view money as it is and change his mind according to the times.

When a purchase is made, the buyer feels that he has gained greater *value* in the goods received than he had in the money he exchanged. Value. That's a key word. It has lots of meanings. Pick one you like. It can mean monetary worth, price, value in exchange for something else, equivalent, cost, rate, amount, expense, charge, etc. It means getting your money's worth. And that can be affected by a thousand circumstances. Timing of your purchase is one of those circumstances.

The key to *value* is *supply* and *demand*. Value depends on who has it and who needs it. If there is more demand than there is supply, then the value is higher. If demand and supply are about even, then the value will remain relatively constant. If there is too much supply and too little demand, the value decreases.

Supply and demand can fluctuate. Let's say you come out with a great new product. At first, all of your neighbors want it. You might even give it away because you just made this thing for fun in the basement. But, no. It catches on. The whole town wants it. You sell whatever you have left, at a little profit. Now the supply is gone.

People bang on your door. They want it. They'll pay for it. You probably say, I was ready to tell the boss off anyway, I might as well spend my time making these things. So you make some more, and you charge more.

Business booms. You buy out your old factory, and you hire the boss as your sales manager. He does a great job. Everyone in the country is crying for your product, and you have a whole warehouse full of it. Supply and demand are about even.

Then the demand begins to fall off. So you have your advertising agency produce a series of nutty commercials, and the demand spurts up for a time. But, because your old boss is such a whiz at selling, he sells one of these things to everyone in the country. You did too good a job on the product. It doesn't wear out. Everyone has one, they are passed from generation to generation, and you can't even give them away.

The supply is great. The demand stinks. The value drops. You've made plenty of money on the thing, so you might just as well forget it. During the process you've managed to accumulate capital, and if you were smart, you took the extra money and you invested it. And chances are good that you'll live happily ever after with the rest of the people in the other 5 per cent.

The above illustration points out how supply and demand can change value. Investments are priced in accordance with the laws of supply and demand, just as goods and services and their values have to follow the laws of supply and demand. Each investment you consider must be judged on its value to you . . . now and in the future. *Now* isn't enough. You have to know what your investment will have as a value in the future. Things might look great now, but what's going to happen in six months, two years, ten years from now? You must be able to project the value of your investment over a period of time. You decide on the time. But know, if possible, what the projected value of your investment will be. And use an accurate, reliable method of determining that future value. If you can jam the necessary facts into a computer, then let it tell you everything possible about the future of the investment before you invest.

This means you have to establish some investment goals. As an investor, you, too, operate on the supply and demand laws. In your case, the goods part of it is money. What's the supply?

What's the demand? If you seem to have too much, then you can afford to invest. If you're a little pressed, your demands are a little high right now, then let the supply catch up.

This becomes a goal. "I've got to have a little more money before I can invest. I know where it's coming from, but it's going to take a little time," you say. Well, set the goals of so much capital in so much time. Then do it.

ESTABLISHMENT OF INVESTMENT GOALS

Life might be a little curious, but it's a wonderful way to see the world. Each of us has twenty-four hours a day for as many days as we're here. It starts with a birthday, and it ends with a death day. Our contribution is measured by what we do during the days between these two days.

We learn goal-seeking early. We take the first step, and then we learn to walk all the way across the room. Most of us don't know it, but we are goal-striving animals. If we don't set out to accomplish something, then usually we *don't* accomplish anything. But we have to set goals. We have to have objectives.

If you're not a goal-setter, then become one. Decide on doing something. Make it simple, at first, and then go after that goal. When you reach it, you do yourself a favor. You make yourself aware of the fact that you can do something. Now set another goal, but make it a little tougher. And rather than just trying to reach it, try to pass it. When you do, you'll be amazed at your ability.

What good is this? Well, it gives you confidence. Let's assume you don't know anything about investments. Your goal must be to learn something about investing or you wouldn't be reading this book. Congratulate yourself. You've just taken that first step. Now we're going to show you how to walk all the way across the room.

You have to have a goal for your money. What do you want your money to do for you? It has been said that money doesn't buy everything but it sure helps to have some. It helps more if the money is at work.

If you just let it rot in the bank, you are wasting your money. And you can use money to help you reach whatever you have set for goals in your life. The two go together. And they can help each other.

Let's say you have a goal to invest. The first thing you have to do is accumulate enough capital to allow you to invest, right? If you don't have enough, make that a goal. Skip the new car this year. Maybe that'll help you reach that particular financial goal a little sooner.

Granted, anyone can stand just so much skimping and saving. But it might be a necessary step in attaining a goal. And when you reach that goal you will realize that it was worth the trouble. While you're on your way toward that goal, have some satisfaction that you are headed exactly where you want to go. Don't cry about not having the new car. Success depends greatly on your attitude.

When an investor has accumulated enough capital to make an investment, the first thing he should do is set another goal. And that goal has to be a definition of what he wants his money to do for him. It could be that this goal will be to establish security. You know, put something aside for a rainy day. Once this has been reached, another goal has to be set immediately. Maybe this will be a goal to make the capital grow to provide for a child's education or for his own retirement.

It doesn't matter to us what you decide on as your financial goals. We've seen just about all of them. We've even seen people who invest just to increase their prestige in the community. It gives the man something to blow about at the club, and it gives his wife a neat little edge at the bridge table. But that's up to them. We don't care if your goals are to accumulate enough capital to travel or play the stock market or buy real estate. The important thing is that you have goals . . . for yourself and for your money.

One man told us that he didn't want large sums of money. He said time with his family and enjoying their relationship were more important to him. His goal was to invest, to grow financially, to be able to control his environment. He wanted to live where he pleased and how he pleased.

It isn't a bad goal. It has a price tag, like any other goal, and he and his wife and their investment counselor determined what that price would be. Then they set out to find a way to reach the goal. Now they are on the way toward it. Sound too easy? Well, friend, it *is* easy.

And a friend of ours told us about one of his real estate investment clients. The man, who was in his forties, wanted security now and in his later years. Between now and then he wanted fine clothes, a big fancy car, he wanted to travel, he wanted to educate his children, and he wanted to be able to sneak off with his wife to a chic resort once in a while. He wanted to be a millionaire. At least he wanted to live like a millionaire. That's a little tougher than the man who wanted to control his environment, but it was absolutely possible in this case.

The goals of the man who wanted to be a millionaire might seem a little unrealistic. It's common for investors to set unrealistic goals. That leads to disappointment. If you set a goal that you know you can't reach, you could frustrate yourself into a terrible mental and financial state.

Also, you must know what to expect from the goals you set. For example, an investor who sets out to provide income for his retirement cannot expect to have much cash income from his investments now. Investments which produce cash in substantial amounts require large amounts of capital invested. That makes sense, doesn't it? All right, then, if capital is to produce large sums of cash in the future, it must be put in growth situations now. This means sacrificing a cash return during the present, in most cases.

Cash income large enough to do the recipient any good is based on the yield and, most important, on the amount of capital invested. Growth builds capital, and large capital can produce large cash income. But few investors should have a goal of immediate cash income if they can't live without investment income and unless they have reached their desired level of capital accumulation.

Earnest investors wanting to accomplish material goals usually can calculate the money needed to satisfy these desires. That's called your price tag on objectives. You can list your goal or goals, and then you can estimate the cost of each. But don't forget that things a few years off probably will cost more than they do today. Let's look at a few examples of long-range goals. Maybe they'll help you figure out the cost of your own.

The objective of the first one is exciting. It's a trip around the world, and let's say the investor wants to go four years from now. What are the facts:

Amount of money needed	$8,000.00
Present available capital	$2,000.00
Additional money available from ordinary income	$1,000.00 (per year)
4 years × $1,000.00	$4,000.00 (direct savings)

This man and his wife have $2,000 to invest. They feel they will be able to save $1,000 a year from the man's income, and, therefore, they will have saved $4,000 in four years. That savings plus the capital adds up to $6,000. They need $2,000 more for the trip, and they want to use their capital of $2,000 to earn the needed $2,000.

This means they would have to invest $2,000 at 25 per cent for four years to be able to attain the goal. The investment capital must therefore be invested to earn a growth or income factor of 25 per cent before figuring compounding interest and after income tax. An investor couldn't possibly expect to earn this kind of return in cautious, fixed rate of return investments such as bonds, mortgages, savings accounts or life insurance.

How will he do it? Only by seeking out high growth investments such as mutual funds, common stock, coins, art or real estate. These can't guarantee the man that the goal will be reached, but they will provide the investor with his only chance of attaining the goal at all.

Let's look at another example. An investor, who is forty years old, wants to retire when he reaches the age of sixty-five, and he wants a $1,000 monthly income at that time.

He has $20,000 to invest.

His investment need goes like this: At the age of sixty-five, the investor wants enough capital to have a very safe investment which yields $12,000 yearly if invested at about 8 per cent per annum. Therefore, capital needed at age sixty-five will be $150,000.

We'll assume that he will not be able to add more capital from his ordinary income, and, therefore, his $20,000 must grow over seven times for him to obtain his goal in twenty-five years.

By calculating the compounding effect, we see that the $20,000 capital would have to be put out to earn *26 per cent* per annum, compounded.

Again, this investment goal can be reached only by going into growth investments and this means assumption of risks necessary to yield 26 per cent per annum. As high as that yield sounds, it is possible for the man to obtain it in commodities, gold, stocks or real estate or some other investment of an equity nature. Risky? Yes. But the only way.

In another example, we see an investor with $200,000 capital at the age of sixty-five. He wants to preserve capital, and he wants to live on the yield. He feels that he needs a net of $1,500 per month from his investments to meet living expenses under his present conditions and desires. His income tax bracket is 30 per cent.

Investment needed: At first, it seems that the investor could simply invest his funds at 9 per cent return to earn the needed $1,500 per month.

$$9 \text{ per cent} \times \$200,000 = \$18,000$$

But he must consider income taxes and inflation trends. At a fixed investment rate of 9 per cent on his money, he would end up with the following:

Yearly gross income from the investment = $18,000
Federal income taxes = $3,600 (30 per cent bracket)
Inflation (12 per cent per year) = $2,160
Actual yield = $12,240 (Actual purchase power)

*[handwritten in margin: / 2 00,000 × 12
= 24,000]*

At the same time, the capital was eroded by $24,000 due to inflation.

Because of the two great bleeders, inflation and taxes, this investor will have to find an investment which presently returns 11.9 per cent in order to truly realize later a 9 per cent yield, plus an additional 12 per cent to keep his capital intact as to purchasing power. Altogether he needs a 24 per cent return.

High growth stocks, commodities, or real estate offer him the best opportunities to reach his goals. And remember, if this investor is to accomplish his goals under present inflationary trends, the fixed rate return type of investments won't work.

Where would you look for investments if you were in his shoes? Of course, conventional investments such as time deposits, certificates, etc., are out. What else might work? Well, maybe rare coins, art or precious metals. Inflation is a real thief.

One more thing to consider is that even leased real estate that is on a fixed return usually won't get the job done unless the lease has a cost tax shelter that bonds, and it will grow in value if the income can be increased periodically to keep pace with inflation.

Let's take another example of investing to reach a specific goal. In this case, a father wants to send his three kids to college. They are ages five, six, and seven. The first one will be in college in about ten years, and the parents have to plan for that right now. Assuming it costs about $10,000 for each student per year, it is going to take $40,000 to send one child to college for four years. And, therefore, the parents can plan on spending three times that, or $120,000.

If the father can invest $30,000 now, it is axiomatic that the money must yield $4,200 yearly after taxes and inflation. This means a net yield of 14 per cent yearly.

In 1967, mutual funds averaged an increase of 15 per cent to 20 per cent. But in the last twenty years, mutuals have only increased 25 per cent. That's only 1.25 per cent per year. However, it is possible that mutual funds could yield the kind of gain the man needs to send his kids to college. One thing in this case is certain. The parents can't even consider investing in conserva-tive, small risk, fixed return investments if they expect to earn enough from their investment to cover the college costs.

Another thing to consider about mutual funds is this. When it is time for the man to use the money for college, the capital will have to be dissipated to meet the expenses. Also, if the invest-ment is sold at the time needed, it will be shrunk by taxes due upon the sale. That's called Capital Gains Tax (shudder).

Consideration of these two points should encourage the inves-tor to seek much higher yields. This could be real estate. Or, if he really likes mutual funds, it would have to be an above average performance mutual fund. But real estate seems to be the logical choice. An average apartment or office building has the ability to produce from 15 per cent to 25 per cent return—after taxes. Now that sounds interesting, doesn't it?

For our last example, we'd like to look at a "wheeler dealer." We'd like to see what a man might do if he wanted to devote his entire life's work to investing.

Actually, he is more than an investor. If you spend all your time investing, then investing is your business. Therefore, the man is a businessman engaged in the business of investing. That changes things quite a bit, according to the IRS. It could make him a dealer, and his tax state would be different than if he were working somewhere else and investing on the side. In other words, his taxes would be based on ordinary rates rather than on the more favorable capital gains (double shudder!).

What are his chances of making a good living and making his estate grow? At best, it's a little rough. But it is being done every day. And it seems as though the road through this kind of life is laced with either gold or despair.

The man might make it in the stock market, but this usually demands a great deal of initial capital. If his Uncle Clyde left him a bundle, the market might be a good place to take it. According to statistics, however, his best chances are in real estate, perhaps as a developer or a subdivider. Real estate offers a great deal of leverage and provides great borrowing power. Either way re-quires one basic quality. You have to be a pro, and you have to have an extra set of guts.

Now you know some of the possibilities offered through wise investing. The first thing to do is to set goals. Then calculate what it's going to take for you to reach the goals. Make a list of the goals, and make a list of what you must be willing to give to reach the goals. This means things like labor, money, risk, etc. Add them up, and you've got a price tag for the goal, and the price tag has to be marked to cover income taxes, inflation, timing and economic conditions.

You can do just one wrong thing. It is the worst thing anyone could ever do, and it ensures failure. You will fail if you do not set goals. You will fail if you don't do anything. Do something. Find an investment that's right for you, and go after it.

Lots of people, just learning about investing, often ask us if there is an ideal goal and an ideal investment. Is there a formula for reaching the ideal through investing? The answer depends on a screwy thing called *you*.

Any investment that allows you to accomplish your goals in the time you set is ideal for you. There isn't any way to measure that until after the goal has been reached, and you can't expect to reach a goal if you don't set one in the first place. After you've decided on the goal, you have to go after it. If you make it, then it's ideal. If you don't, maybe the goal was a little too tough. But you will not completely fail if you do something. You will fail— you will wind up in the 95 per cent—only if you don't do anything at all.

We feel that an investment must be tailored to individual needs, goals, resources, capabilities and temperament. Investing isn't a general subject. Lots of people think it is, however, and they illustrate their ignorance by saying things like, "Real estate is a rich man's game," or "Only the guys with lots of money can play the stock market." There are fantastic opportunities for everyone in both. You can buy a share of stock for just about any price. You can invest in real estate for much less than you thought.

Also, we'd like to get it straight here that an investor can seldom rely on one medium of investing to satisfy his goals. Most of the success stories on investments show a combination of investments. If you don't know a whole lot about investing, then you ought to hook up with a reliable real estate investment counselor. He spends his time right in the middle of the field of investing, and he knows more about the opportunities than you do.

All he needs to know about you is simply everything. He needs to know your resources, your goals, your income, your standard of living, your wife and your kids. He needs a complete financial history on you, and he needs to know where you want to go and at what speed. Then he'll weigh some facts for you, and he'll make some recommendations.

It's possible that he'll say forget it. But that's unlikely. Probably he'll tell you what it will take to make the goals, and he'll be able to help you determine the price tag more accurately. He'll help you explore all of the possibilities. And the combination of investments, not *the* investment, which could be ideal for you.

Then you can get after it. You can put your money to work, and it will work for you night and day . . . even while you're asleep.

CHAPTER 4

GUIDELINES FOR EVALUATING AN INVESTMENT

You can't just rush headlong into investing. You need to use a magnifying glass and a scale, and you need to be able to examine the investment thoroughly before you act. You wouldn't buy a car without kicking the tires, blowing the horn, looking under the hood, and you wouldn't buy a house without seeing every room and knocking on the walls.

It would be fun to skip through life tossing your money here and there, hoping for the best and not being sure of anything, wouldn't it? Lots of people do that. They're in that grim 95 per cent today.

The smart guys were careful, but in a different way from the others. They knew that investing was the way to become rich, but they were exact and a little cunning. They were out to avoid the failure game so many of us play. The goals probably were similar. Probably they wanted success.

Success doesn't mean massive wealth. Success in life means doing what you want to do, living as comfortably as you want to live, and reaching those goals you have set for yourself. There are many successful people who are not rich. And that goes for all ages, not just the sixty-five and over class.

Some people like the pressures of business. Others like the freedom of little responsibility in their jobs. Some would rather spend their time working than pulling up the crab grass. Some want the big, fancy cars, and others could care less about even owning a car. Status? What's that?

Status is a thing the neighbors and the community and the club impose on us. It makes life more competitive, and competition breeds accomplishment. But we like the people who are individuals. They could care less about keeping up with the Joneses, and, as a matter of fact, they didn't even realize that the Joneses had a new car until the Joneses pointed it out to them.

The successful people are not those who try to attain success just to show off to the rest of the world. They are the people who attain what they set out to attain because that's what they wanted to attain. They did it for themselves. And, sure, that makes for pride, and it feels good to have everyone know that you are a success. But you're the guy who has to be convinced. You know why? Because no one else usually gives a damn.

Envy and admiration are a little alike. But envy is wanting to be something else. You can envy someone else, but when you really sit down to evaluate the person's position, would you really like to be where he is, doing what he does? Possibly. But you don't know exactly how he got there, and if you did, you might not want that set of problems.

Admiration is a compliment. You can say, "Gee, old Charlie really has it made," and you can feel good about it if you admire Charlie. If you envy him, you could hate everything about him. Envy is like inflation. It eats you alive.

Selecting goals, then, can't be based on envy of someone else's success. You have to be an individual about your goals. You can't set out to attain someone else's goals. Those goals are their goals, and they are based on an entirely different set of circumstances. You have to weigh your goals, and you have to decide on them—and what they'll do for you—before you set out after them. Investing is a way to get there, but, as we said, you have to weigh the investments before you commit yourself.

There are seven basic factors to consider when you are trying to decide which course of action to take in investing. They are risk, yield, growth, management, liquidity, predictability and tax shelter. And to weigh each of these, you have to know what each involves. Let's tackle them one at a time.

RISK

In the true meaning of the word, to us, anyway, investment has an element of risk. The degree of risk ranges all the way from slight to great, but it does exist. If no risk is involved, then it is likely that there will be no chance for profit. And since you invest for profit, you have to accept the fact that an investment has some risk.

Take a big chance, if you want to, and the rewards could be great. Greater chances for profit exist with greater degrees of risk. And the greater the risk, the greater the chance of losing your profit, your capital and your mind.

Sometimes risk is sneaky. It is a hidden factor. Something might attract you because it seems to have little or no risk involved. A hint to hidden risk is the profit factor. You and we know that you can't expect something for nothing. Look carefully before you leap.

Savings. Do savings accounts exhibit risk? Insurance. Do cash value insurance policies have any risk?

In 1976, depositors in savings and life insurance reserves *lost* an estimated $1½ billion. Well, Andy, there must be a little risk involved in these two safe forms of investing. The loss can be blamed on a loss in purchase power or inflation. Look at this example.

Ten years ago, $10,000 in a savings account earned 4 per cent interest each year. That sounds okay, but what about the inflation rate? If the inflation rate was 2 per cent, then the actual return on the money invested in the 4 percent savings account was really only 2 per cent. And then, what about income taxes on the earnings? The plot thickens, right?

If the tax bracket was high enough, or if the rate of inflation was more than 2 per cent, there may have been an actual loss of the principal and its capacity to buy goods. That's sneaky. And that's hidden risk, namely inflation. The nature of fixed return investments is damned by not being able to keep up with inflation. Today's inflation is 9 to 18 per cent depending on what dummy governmental agency is doing the calculating.

A list of common types of fixed rate return investments includes bonds, savings accounts, life insurance cash values, mortgages and notes or commercial paper.

Risk has to be considered when you make an investment. Timing, trends and the types of investments determine the degree of risk. Some risks are apparent, such as loss of market, deterioration, competition and others. But the hidden risks are harder to understand. However, the risk is just as real. And there is only one 100 per cent risk, and that's investing in something that cannot possibly reach your goals or not doing anything about investing at all.

Calculation of risk is complicated. Statistics help, and the most valuable statistics are called *chance of success* and *per cent of failure*. These statistics are available from many sources, including the Federal Government. But you can get these and other statistics from suppliers, manufacturers, libraries and research organizations. Look in the Yellow Pages.

The statistics guide us to *the odds* on success or failure of the investment. But we have to study cycles, trends, economic conditions, past history and prognostications to help us determine the chances of success or failure in the venture. This should ram home the point of knowing what you are doing before you do it in investing. And you can see, too, that you might learn something from a professional real estate investment counselor. He knows what you need to know before you make the investment, and he has many, many sources of information not available to the layman.

There is a formula, however, you can use to rate the chances of success for your investment, but the factors in the formula have to be backed up with research on the specific investment you are considering. And all of this can't give you a definite, final word to determine the actual risk involved in the investment. You sort of have to feel your way. How does it look to you? Measure it by deciding in your own mind the personal risk you will be assuming by making the proposed investment. Weigh your personal liability, age, health, available resources. These are important factors in determining risk. You have to make the final decision.

Wise fiscal planning tells us to set goals. We can expect some risk by investing, but the greatest risk of all is lack of action.

Look at the 95 per cent of the 19 million people surveyed by the Kennedy Administration. They played it safe. Did they take any risk? They decided on the 100 per cent risk, in most cases. They didn't do anything, and, as a result, they ended up not having a whole lot to show for it. Did the other 5 per cent take a chance or two? Yes. What did it get them? Financial independence, that's all.

Some make it, and some don't. That's easy to accept, but it isn't so easy to understand why. You can't just say flatly that those who didn't make it didn't save up for the later years. In fact, 95 per cent of them did save. Most of them bought cash reserve life insurance. At the time of the survey, which was taken in 1960, the American public had approximately $127 billion in life insurance reserves. It might seem safe, but according to the survey, 95 per cent of us could be broke at the age of sixty-five. That's *living risk*.

Let's say you have set a goal of having $100,000 saved by the time you are sixty-five. If you save it in fixed return investments which erode faster than they earn, you can't possibly make it . . . regardless of the original investment even up to $100,000.

Since this book is about real estate investing as a way to get rich while sleeping, we'll take this opportunity to mention risk in real estate. The range in real estate risk goes all the way from extremely low to outright gambling. We told you real estate had broad possibilities. And a risk range of safe to insane is about as broad as you can get.

The stock market has about the same range. Real estate can offer categories of risk equal to just about anything on the stock market. For example, a corporate or government bond has little obvious risk, and they are available on the market. Not to be outdone, real estate offers property leased by the government or AAA credit-rated corporations. These, too, have little obvious risk.

"Penny" or very cheap stock can have about the same degree of risk as small parcels of raw land way off the path of progress. Apartment buildings and office buildings hold no more risk than the average listed common stock or over-the-counter securities.

Selection of the investment has to do with your own goals. Once you establish meaningful goals, determine the risk, and then see if the risk affects your goal attainment. The only way to miss is to be too cautious or too careless. Compare all of the possibilities, and don't hesitate to use a combination.

Oh, the formula? It's easy. Decide on the goal. Investigate the investment that will get you there on time. Decide how much risk you can stand. Alter the goal if necessary, but don't shut it out completely. Then go after it. Let your money work for you.

YIELD

The most common use of the word *yield* is on yellow signs at freeway entrances. In that sense it means give up. We're talking about a different kind of yield. Our yield means *get*.

Every investment is supposed to produce a yield, and it comes in several different forms. Yield can be growth, cash, tax savings . . . even all three. Yield can be affected by trends, inflation or deflation and taxes. Yield, sometimes called return, usually is in direct proportion to risk.

The first thing to consider when investing is the preservation of your capital. Without capital, you can't invest. And watch out for hidden risks or apparent risks. If you select a fixed rate or return on your capital, you stand to make a greater return when the economy is on a deflation kick. The opposite is true in periods of inflation.

Return can be obtained in three basic ways. One is income,

which means interest, dividends, operating income, rents, etc. Another is growth, which means buying low and selling high, appreciation, increase in demand and decrease in supply. The third is tax shelter. Tax shelter is a legal means of saving on income tax, which produces a saving of income.

When considering a return on investment, you will consider the three types of income, and you will calculate the total return you can expect while continuing to preserve your capital.

There are three types of income from every investment.

1. Taxable (a tax liability or a tax shelter);
2. Net spendable (actual cash left for your pocket after taxes have been paid);
3. Equity (can be growth or loss).

True income or yield is the total of the three types of income from the investment. Add 'em up. The result is the true income from the investment.

Let's look at an example, and let's say we're investigating the possible advantages of purchasing a tax exempt bond. The face of the bond says it will return 5 per cent and it costs $1,000 or par for it.

Question: What's the true net yield in today's economic situation with inflation at 10 per cent?

Expected gross yield (5 per cent × $1,000)	= $50.00
Add growth (non-likely)	$00.00
Add tax shelter	$00.00
Subtotal	$50.00
Loss of purchase power due to 10 per cent inflation (10 per cent × $1,000)	−$100.00
True net yield	−$50.00

Therefore, this means we will actually lose $50.00 this year on the investment. Here is proof that apparent yield is often not true, because all factors haven't been taken into account by most investors.

GROWTH

A true investment must show some kind of activity. Hopefully that activity will be on the up trend, and when it is, the investment has growth. To do you any good, an investment must have growth. Something has to result from your effort, and your money can't waste its time. A true investment yields something significant only if it shows growth. It's kind of like planting a seed. You expect a bean or a flower.

But you have to give the seed a chance. It needs good soil, water, sunshine, care. That's the way with investments, too. They need care, and they need a chance to grow. Too bad you can't plant a dime and get a dime tree, and too bad you can't plant a hundred dollar bush and get hundred dollar bills after the thing blooms.

But, like plants, the climate can be just right for investment growth. This is determined by supply and demand and the true economic climate, which can be described as inflation or deflation. Also, you'll want to look at the track record of the investment. What has it done in the past? How was its growth? How does the future look, based on the past history? You need to know all of this.

Growth is an extremely important factor, and much depends on how much management will be required if you make the investment. Remember that all-important supply and demand—it makes or breaks growth.

MANAGEMENT

Like risk, management can be obvious and it can be hidden. Not all investments are management free, and there are such things as primary and secondary management to consider. An example of this is when an investor completes his research and decides to buy into a real estate syndication. When he buys, he is exercising primary or initial money management. But once the investor's money is placed, it will be the responsibility of the syndication to carry out the management duties concerning the money and the property. That's called secondary management.

Just as you have to determine risk, you have to rate the degree of management you are willing to exert in the life of your investment. Poor management can ruin a seemingly good investment, and the secret is to make sure your investment is managed properly. If you can't do it, then get someone who can. It would be better to pay a professional manager than to try to save a little money and wind up goofing the thing because you aren't capable of being the manager. Good management usually brings good results. Bad management usually brings bad results.

Nearly every kind of investment requires a degree of management. It might be as simple as keeping your savings book up to date, which the bank will do for you. And it could be as involved as managing an apartment house.

As an investor, you will make the decision on how your investment will be managed. If the risk seems about right, and if the returns you expect seem about right, and if you feel that you can handle the investment without outside help, you are welcome to the labor of managing the investment. It can be fun. Lots of people like to be involved that deeply with their investments. Others, on the other hand, don't even want to see anything about the investments except the results.

Pure investment is when the capital, not the investor, does the work. But this isn't too common. In the most pure of pure investments, the kind where you don't have to do anything, you still have to think about the investment once in a while. That's a form of management.

The decision boils down to your own likes or dislikes or availability or unavailability for the management duties. But someone has to watch over the investment. You rate it. But be a little modest about your own abilities.

LIQUIDITY

Hard, cold cash is pure liquidity. It's great to have lots of cash, but it usually isn't classified as an investment. Some people, however, do speculate or invest in currency and they try to take advantage of varying exchange ratios in foreign currency. It isn't exactly rare, but it isn't too common. Those who do this are real pros.

Liquidity means the ability to convert an investment to ready cash, and each investment has a different degree of liquidity. To be of value to the investor, the investment must be transferable to another person. Growth depends entirely on liquidity. This is true because an investor cannot take advantage of appreciation until the investment is liquidated in the form of cash. Also, borrowing is a form of liquidity.

There must be an availability of a market which creates liquidity. The investor considers it essential to be able to sell an investment, reach liquidity and then reinvest if he wants to reinvest.

Commonly known investments can be rated as to a degree of timely liquidity as follows:

1. Savings accounts
2. Government securities
3. Life insurance cash values or reserves
4. Listed bonds
5. Listed stocks
6. Mortgages and notes
7. Real estate

If you invest in savings, all you have to do is go to the bank and make a withdrawal. Real estate, on the other end of the liquidity scale, requires a sale of property or an exchange of property. This takes a little longer than making out a withdrawal slip at the friendliest bank in town.

Each of the magnificent seven investments has internal degrees of liquidity. The bank might be closed, for example, and you might have to wait until Monday to get your money. And it's possible that the bank might have to make you wait. Your account is full, let's say, and you want the full $15,000 plus interest. It might take them a while to scrape up enough to pay you off.

Old number seven, real estate, has different degrees of liquidity, too. Properties leased to AAA credit-rated firms, and priced at market value, can be liquidated faster than a store with so-so credit-rated tenants, in most cases.

Price usually isn't determined by a seller of stocks. He takes what he can get in the market on the day of the sale. If real estate were priced in the same manner, there would be immediate liquidity in real estate. Real estate is the only one of the sacred seven that often isn't priced at going quotations as of the date of the sale. Often, real estate isn't marketed at cash sale prices. And each piece of real estate is unique. There might be others similar to it, but none is exactly like another, and each must be valued as to its return or use possibilities. We don't like to knock real estate, but it's true that real estate isn't rapidly liquid unless it is priced to sell at the going rate. That's okay if you're a buyer, but what if you're a seller? You want the best price, naturally, and it might take a while to find someone who is willing to pay your outrageous price. Take a look at this little illustration. It shows how terms also effect liquidity of real estate:

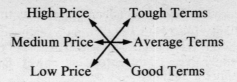

High Price   Tough Terms

Medium Price ⟷ Average Terms

Low Price   Good Terms

Good terms usually mean a higher degree of liquidity even at a higher selling price. Simply stated, it takes longer to transfer real estate than it does to transfer other forms of investments.

There are two ways to gain liquidity. You can sell, or you can borrow. The rule is this: The greater amount of money you can borrow on an asset, the more liquidity it has or offers. Time, of course, is a factor. In selling an investment speed is supposed to be good for the owner.

Often, liquidity is overrated. Lots of investors place great importance on liquidity because they believe that the investment can be good only if it can be cashed in quickly. That isn't always true.

But liquidity is important. If an investor sees adverse conditions building, it can cloud the future. He might decide to liquidate his investment before the expected condition becomes a reality. Also, when a better opportunity presents itself, the investor may want to liquidate his present investments to take advantage of the new opportunity.

Some investors want a high degree of liquidity so that they can operate on short term borrowed money. We think these are the big gamblers. Many are successful, but we certainly don't recommend this kind of operation to you if this is your first exposure to investing.

There's one other very important reason for liquidity. Suppose you complete your research on an investment, weigh all of the factors, take our advice and listen to your investment counselor, your wife, your postman and your boss. You decide, by God, that's the thing to buy. You don't know why exactly, but it feels good. Everything looks okay, give or take a couple of factors, and you dive into it because you just know it's going to be absolutely marvelous.

Something goes wrong, or something happens that makes you go sour on the whole deal. Well, what do you want? You want your money. How fast can you get it back? That's liquidity, and it's a simple reason for having liquidity.

Liquidity has a price tag on it. Most non-fixed return investments have a high degree of liquidity, and they have an explosive price index. The price of these assets is subject to rapid change (e.g., the Stock Market). Also, high liquidity assets don't give the investor a chance to sit back to see what's really going on in that particular market. Buying and selling can be lots of fun, but it can be awfully expensive. Time, borrowing power and motive are deciding factors for liquidity.

Back up your decision on liquidity requirements by making a study of the average time required to sell the investment you are considering. Also, find out the amount of a loan readily obtained from a lender on your proposed investment.

PREDICTABILITY

Can you predict the results of your investment? Can you conduct an analysis and project what your investment will do in the future . . . and then back it up with facts? Or is investing like shooting craps?

If you were able to predict your earnings from a spree in Las Vegas, then you could con your wife into believing that you were going on a three-night, one-day investment trip to Las Vegas. The places over there are called gambling casinos. Chance is the key word. The only predictable thing about Las Vegas is that the gambling casinos are going to win.

You can be a little more sophisticated than that with your investments. If you're not, in fact, then you might as well go to Las Vegas. Ask a loser, either someone in the investment game or the crap game, if he enjoyed giving his money away. There's only one answer. No.

In a little while we're going to show you how you can use some specialized tools to make accurate predictions on real estate investments for the next five, ten, even twenty years. It is tangible predictability, and it makes Las Vegas look like the sham that it is.

Oh, they do have a new offer. And they have a prediction to make, too. The Las Vegas boys predict that if you bring your investment capital to them on a first class seat of a jet, they'll send you home after a few days of "investing" with them in a $130,000 limousine. We checked it out. The limo is a Greyhound Bus.

TAX SHELTER

The Supreme Court gives us a break. They say, ". . . It is the right of the citizenry to pay the least amount of taxes possible." Great. What does it mean? It used to be that a tax expert could be called in to tell us what the government means when they talk about taxes. Then the specialists had to specialize. One had to ask another before an answer that couldn't be understood was offered. We don't have tax experts anymore. It's impossible to keep up with all of the changes. All we have now is a group of people who are called tax experts, but in reality, they are people with varying degrees of ignorance on the subject.

Tax shelter is important, and it isn't too hard to understand. We placed it last on the list of guidelines because of its importance and because it is the last thing you should do when judging an investment for yourself.

So many investments advertise the general public to death and into believing and thinking only about return on the investment. This kind of brainwashing presents false facts.

Look at a couple of examples:

A STOCK

Bought at	$1,000
Sold at	$1,200
Return	20%?

BONDS

Bought at	$1,000
Interest	8%
Return	$80?

SAVINGS ACCOUNT

Deposit	$1,000
Interest	6%
Return	$60?

The man with the stock said, "I made 20 per cent." The man with the bonds said, "I made 8 per cent." The woman with the savings account said, "I made 6 per cent."

They are kidding themselves. It's like saying you earn $25,000 a year at your job, and, therefore, you can live on $25,000 a year. Right? Wrong! Two years of that, and you'd be in the pen for nonpayment of $6,800 in taxes.

It isn't important, according to our way of thinking, how much

you make. It doesn't mean a thing to us. We're not impressed with
your salary . . . regardless of how large it might be. What's
important? You need to know how much of that wad you can
keep. "Keep money," we call it. And to us it makes a whole lot
more sense.

"Keep money" is the return on your investment after taxes.
And the way to have more keep money is through tax shelter. We
have devoted an entire section of the book to keep money and tax
shelter.

We'll say this about it now. Real estate offers more tax shelter
opportunities than any other form of investment. It's a method of
keeping money that you would have to pay to the government in
taxes in other investment situations.

Remember the guidelines to investment. They are Risk, Yield,
Growth, Management, Liquidity, Predictability and Tax Shelter.
Know what makes up each. Know how to use information to
determine the weight of each of these decision-making factors
. . . before you invest in anything.

CHAPTER 5

COMPARISON OF INVESTMENTS

We suggested earlier that for you to judge an investment, you
have to weigh the factors involved in risk, yield, growth, management, liquidity, predictability and tax shelter. These are the
standards by which any investment is understood. By using the
information on possible investments, you can compare the good
and bad points of any of them with any others.

You can compare one stock with another, and you can compare
one property with another. You can compare a stock with a real
estate property, and so on. In fact, you must compare the investments you are considering.

You cannot, however, compare general classifications of investment media. As you know, every life insurance policy has
different aspects to consider. And you, as a prospective buyer,
should compare all the available insurance contracts before you
buy. That's the theory, of course, and things like, "Well, I buy
from George because he's my brother-in-law . . ." can't intrude
into this kind of comparison.

But we like George, too, and he represents a fairly good company. And we know as well as you that the average buyer of life insurance doesn't have the time or the knowledge to go into the details on a thousand different policies available today. There are all sorts of charts and services and other information available to anyone interested in buying life insurance, but for the most part these tend to confuse rather than reveal. The insurance salesmen know this, and they make a pitch on what they think you'll go for as far as premiums and so on are concerned.

Just as you should use the knowledge of a qualified investment counselor if you don't know how to invest, you should be able to rely on a trustworthy fellow like George when you buy insurance.

This fits today's pattern, and it's a good idea to ask someone who knows before you do almost anything. There are specialists in every field—medicine, law, insurance, real estate, etc., and payment for their services usually is a bargain. A little later in the book we'll tell you how to select an investment counselor. You can compare this with the way you select a doctor or the way you select a lawyer.

In regard to the comparison of investments, however, you have learned something already. You know that money is a tool, and you know how that tool can work for you. You know that the first step in investing means that you have to accumulate enough capital to invest. Then, as you know, the next step is to set some goals, and you will have to determine if you can afford the price tags on those goals.

We have explored the basic elements of an investment with you, and we've given you some tips on how to judge each investment you might consider.

So this places you at a point of action. You've got the money, the goals. You're itching to move on something. What will it be? That's where comparison of investments comes in. What do you compare? You compare those factors used to judge any investment—Risk, Yield, Growth, Management, Liquidity, Predictability and Tax Shelter. And you rate each of these elements for each investment considered. The resulting rates give you scores in numerical form. Then you can compare them, and it's a snap to see which investment offers the best score.

We have selected some possible investments, just to show you how the method works, but you can use these formulas to compare any investment you consider in the future. We've used Savings Accounts, Commodities, Stocks, Mutuals, Bonds, Art and Miscellaneous Investments, Insurance, Mortgages and, of course, Real Estate. Each of the seven judgment elements is taken in order.

RISK

Assumptions: These ratings will change according to economic conditions. The following comparisons were made during a time when inflation was at 8 per cent.

You have to use your own understanding of economic conditions at the time you are making these comparisons. Remember, your knowledge and understanding is probably as good as the expert's!

What are the chances that the original investment may end up a loss? Sure to lose? Give it a 0. Sure to win? Give it a 10. (Consider inflation and deflation.)

10 = excellent
 0 = poor

Savings Account	Stocks	Mutuals	Comm.	Bonds	Art Misc.	Ins.	Mrtg.	Real Estate
2	4	4	5	2	5	0	2	9

YIELD (Income)

True yield is figured after taxes and less an allowance for inflation. Only income counts in this section.

0 = least
10 = most

Yield expressed in % returns	Savings Account	Stocks	Mutuals	Comm.	Bonds	Art	Ins.	Mrtg.	Real Estate	Rating
no income				X		X				0
Less than 3%	X				X		X	X		2
3–4%										4
4–6%		X	X				X			6
6–10%								X		8
over 10%									X	10
Points	2	6	6	0	2	0	2	2	10	

GROWTH

Is there likelihood of growth?

No! Rate it 0.

Absolutely! Rate it 10.

Rating: 0–10

Savings Account	Stocks	Mutuals	Comm.	Bonds	Art Misc.	Ins.	Mrtgs.	Real Estate
0	5	5	5	2	7	0	1	9

MANAGEMENT

Percent of Time and Talent Required of Investors	Rating Point
100%	0
90%	1
80%	2
70%	3
60%	4
50%	5
40%	6
30%	7
20%	8
10%	9
10% or less	10

Rating: 0–10

Savings Account	Stocks	Mutuals	Comm.	Bonds	Art Misc.	Ins.	Mrtg.	Real Estate
10	7	9	7	9	4	9	7	5

LIQUIDITY   (Part I)

Formula
for Salability

Length of time needed to convert to cash

1 Week or less	10
1 Month or less	5
3 Months or less	3
Longer	0

If there is any loss of original investment, deduct half the points.

Savings Account	Stocks	Mutuals	Comm.	Bonds	Art Misc.	Ins.	Mrtg.	Real Estate
10	10	10	10	10	3	10	3	3

During a dire emergency—depression of 1929-1939—insurance companies closed their *pay-out* windows but not the *pay-in* windows for six months. Check your policy. The insurance companies may take up to six months to pay out your cash values in case of surrendering your policy or if your intent is to borrow them in an emergency. Also, some banks closed.

LIQUIDITY   (Part II)

BORROWABILITY

Borrowing Percentage	Rating Point
Can borrow less than 10% of value	0
Can borrow 10% of value	1
Can borrow 20% of value	2
Can borrow 30% of value	3
Can borrow 40% of value	4
Can borrow 50% of value	5
Can borrow 60% of value	6
Can borrow 70% of value	7
Can borrow 80% of value	8
Can borrow 90% of value	9
Can borrow 100% of value	10

TOTAL POINT RATING

Savings Account	Stocks	Mutuals	Comm.	Bonds	Art Misc.	Ins.	Mrtg.	Real Estate
10	5	5	9	9	2	10	6	7

The liquidity formula must be backed up by statistics on the average time required to sell, and also by the amount of a loan that can be obtained readily from a willing lender.

For example, the purchasing of stocks on margin is required by the government. If the margin is 20%, for instance, a stock purchaser would have a (Part I) liquidity rating of 2. Since most listed stock can be sold in 10 days or less, the Part II rating would be 10. The average liquidity rating is 6 (2 + 10 = 12 ÷ 2 = 6).

TOTAL LIQUIDITY

0 = Most time needed (to cash in)
10 = Least time needed (to cash in)

	Savings Account	Stocks	Mutuals	Comm.	Bonds	Art Misc.	Ins.	Mrtg.	Real Estate
Borrowable	10	5	5	9	9	2	10	3	7
Saleable	10	5	5	10	10	3	5	3	3
Total Points	20	10	10	19	19	5	15	6	10
Average	10	5	5	9	9	2	7	3	5

PREDICTABILITY

How accurately can you predict the growth and yield of your investments within a five- or ten-year period? (Consider inflation and taxes.)

0 = None
10 = Maximum

Rating: 0–10

Savings Account	Stocks	Mutuals	Comm.	Bonds	Art Misc.	Ins.	Mrtg.	Real Estate
8	4	4	1	6	1	5	8	8

TAX SHELTER

To what degree does your investment
have tax shelters?

0 = None
10 = Maximum

Rating: 0–10

Savings Account	Stocks	Mutuals	Comm.	*Bonds	Art Misc.	Ins.	Mrtg.	Real Estate
0	0	0	0	0	4	0	0	10

*Unless tax exempt; then the rating will be 10.

We have applied the formulas to each of the investments under consideration. We have rated all the elements of an investment, and now we can collect them and place them on the "BIG BOARD" for final evaluation.

	Savings Account	Stocks	Mutuals	Comm.	Bonds	Art Misc.	Ins.	Mrtg.	Real Estate
Risk	2	4	4	5	2	5	0	2	9
Yield	2	6	6	0	2	0	2	2	10
Growth	0	5	5	5	2	7	0	1	9
Management	10	7	9	7	9	4	9	7	5
Liquidity	10	5	5	9	9	2	7	3	5
Predictability	8	4	4	1	6	1	5	8	8
Tax shelter	0	0	0	0	0	4	0	0	10
TOTAL	32	31	33	27	30	23	24	23	56

Perfect Score = 70

Conclusions:

1. Risks: All "fixed dollar returns" show the least risk. Of the four with the least amount of risk, three of them also have the least yield. This is true for all "fixed return" investments.
2. Yield: We see proof that when you are looking for income, the primary investment is real estate.
3. Growth: The "fixed returns" with the least risk and least "yield" have the least growth.
4. Management: This shows us the difference between stocks and mutuals.
5. Liquidity: Liquidity depends on the individual investor's needs, his willingness to take a loss, and current values.
6. Predictability: It's easy to predict fixed returns, but only one growth and yield investment can be predictable—real estate.
7. Tax Shelter: Only one investment stands head and shoulders above the field for potential tax shelter—real estate.

CHAPTER 6

ANALYSIS OF COMPARISION RATINGS OF SAVINGS ACCOUNTS, MUTUAL FUNDS, STOCKS, ART, THE COMMODITY MARKET

With the information we obtained in our research, and then converted to actual ratings through the use of our comparative formulas, we are now in a better position to conduct an analysis of the investments we have considered.

Let's take them one at a time, and let's look into each to study the types and purposes of each of the investments. Also, note the rating score of each.

SAVINGS ACCOUNTS   Score _32_

Commercial banks, savings and loan associations and credit unions make up the majority of institutions which offer savings account facilities. The purpose of a savings account is to provide an immediate source of cash to meet emergencies. Also, it is to provide an intermediate place to accumulate cash before it is put to a better use. A good rule of thumb for the maximum amount of money one should have in savings is one year of living expenses.

Although a savings account is a vital portion of one's financial planning, it becomes overdone when any amount of money over what is needed for emergencies is locked in a vault. The return paid by savings institutions is low. The institution makes a greater return on your money by putting the funds into areas that are considered more of an investment. Of course, the risk to the saver is very low.

Wise fiscal planning dictates that you have some ready resources and the liquidity offered by the savings account. But don't forget its real purpose. A savings account is your true emergency fund. A savings account is not a true investment. In 1929, John J. Raskob said, "No one can become rich merely by saving." We agree.

The gamble-proof way to double your money.

There aren't too many sure things in this world. Double-Your-Money certificates, guaranteed to pay two dollars for every dollar you invest in just 13 years and 11 months. This is based on a guaranteed 5% interest rate. If prevailing rates go above that figure, you're always free to withdraw your savings—on any 90-day anniversary of purchase—with interest paid to that date. The option is yours . . . the commitment is all ours. You can't lose with gamble-proof Double-Your-Money certificates.

How your money grows with Double-Your-Money Certificates				
	1 year	5 years	10 years	13 years 11 months
$ 50	$ 52.55	$ 64.20	$ 82.45	$100.28
$100	105.11	128.40	164.89	200.57
$200	210.22	256.80	329.78	401.14

Double-Your-Money Certificates guarantee to pay 5% interest, compounded daily for thirteen years, eleven months.

This type of ad is running rampant throughout the country and lets the depositor believe he is doubling his money in 13 years, 11 months—but, like the rest of the 95 per cent, no allowance has been made for the ever-present inflation factor, and ever-ever-present tax deduction on earned money. Now just what does that "doubling your money" really amount to?

MUTUAL FUNDS   Score _33_

There is much similarity in the real estate syndicate and the mutual fund. Both use the principle of not putting all your eggs in one basket. Mutual funds have become one of America's most popular investments with about $73 billion in assets. The rest of the world is following suit.

Since the inception of mutuals, American public insurance companies, pension funds, etc., have invested billions. Generally speaking, these funds have served their stockholders very well. Mutual funds have enjoyed substantial growth.

The real purpose of mutual funds, for the investor, is growth. While the average yield of mutuals in 1966 was 3.9 per cent, it is obvious that the investor seeking substantial yearly income from yield did not achieve this goal. Most funds are not designed to provide yearly cash income or yield. Some feel that by selling off the shares that represent the capital growth, the investor can obtain a fair return or yield in cash. Remember, however, when this is done, any gain will be taxed. Of course, we realize that the yield or gain will have the favorable tax rate of capital gains if held for the correct period of time.

Much has been written about the mechanics, advantages and disadvantages of mutual funds. Any interested investor can find plenty of information if he wants it. But remember this: the best features of the mutual fund are very little management, diversification, good liquidity, and some possibility of growth. Disadvantages are failure to keep up with inflation, low yield, very little tax shelter, and slightly less leverage than some other investments offer.

An investor going into mutual funds as an investment should weigh the advantages and disadvantages to determine if mutuals suit his purpose. The investor who must live on income from his investments, or the person in a high income tax bracket who is still paying too much tax, should look elsewhere. Most mutual funds are not the ticket for these people.

Small investors inexperienced in management of stock portfolios, who want a chance for growth and low risk, and who are not concerned with income taxes or cash returns—for these investors the mutual fund could be the proper investment. The basic and primary original selling feature of mutual funds was the introduction of professional management for the average investor. This made him a passive investor, and it eliminated one of the biggest problems of investing in the stock market. The small or occasional investor could depend on someone else's management knowledge.

Mutual funds, further, started out to deliver assured growth through diversification, and they had a remarkable record until everyone wanted to become a Fund Manager with the fabulous returns of the management fee. Experienced, inexperienced, financial wizards, hot shots and overnight geniuses became Fund Managers. The number of funds has recently decreased remarkably. At this printing, there are approximately 780 different funds available. Twelve years ago there were about 1600 mutual funds. All of them are fighting and competing for the small and large investor dollar. They want the wage earner, the profit sharing trust, union trust, and pension dollar, and the bait they use is called performance or Track Record.

Naturally, this forces many of these "Funds" to do tricks to obtain sales. Trying to qualify these different funds by looking at and studying their former potent selling point of management becomes increasingly difficult. But we do have a barometer upon which we can evaluate these different funds. They ask us to judge them by their performance. Okay, judge away.

Ten thousand dollars invested in mutual funds in 1967 grew to $17,768 by 1975. Big whoop! That is less than 10 per cent a year. What has mutual fund professional management meant to the small investor? Very little. It has put him back to the same gambling, speculative position he was in when trying to pick a winner in the stock market. Choose your fund carefully.

STOCKS—SECURITIES   Score _31_

Everything that we have said about mutual funds generally applies to the stock market. The major differences add up to this: Going into the stock market, as an individual investor, you usually give up the management skills and diversification shelter offered by mutual funds. This does not mean that going into the general stock market isn't good, but it does mean that you must have a good broker to advise you, or you must be astute and knowledgeable yourself. This can require more management by you if you go into the market by yourself.

As far as inflation, growth, liquidity, etc., is concerned, the funds and the general market are much alike. The purpose of the stock market and the mutual fund is the same for the investor. Do not expect high leverage, yearly cash income exceeding an average of 4.62 per cent, or much tax shelter out of the general stock market. If your individual stock did as well as the Dow Jones Industrial Average, your $10,000 investment in 1967 grew to only $10,848 by 1975. It does offer investors good advantages—IF THEY FIT YOUR PURPOSE—for making the investment.

BONDS   Score _30_

One big thing the stock market offers is bonds and convertible bonds, preferred stocks and other securities that have fixed yields. Since we have already discussed investments with fixed returns and their disadvantages as to inflation and taxes, it is not necessary for us to go into it again. One thing we will say, however, is that some convertible bonds have advantages few other investments have. This is fixed returns and the possibility of growth as well.

Bonds are loans made to a company, and the financial strength of the company issuing the bonds will determine risk. Many financial experts agree that bonds issued at the going rate of return which can be converted into the common stock of a growing company are high up on the list of good investments. Other than the disadvantage of not offering tax shelter, convertible bonds can be an excellent way to accumulate wealth.

It can be said that the purpose of issuing convertible bonds is to borrow funds at a usually lower fixed rate of return, yet offer a security that can keep pace with inflation and thus offer the possibility of growth through conversion to common stock. However, persons in need of tax shelter on their ordinary income will not find the regular bond or the convertible bond the answer. Also, the investor seeking immediate income may not find the convertible bond the right answer because a highly rated convertible bond usually will yield 1 per cent to ½ per cent below the regular bond market. The reason for this is that the company issuing the bond will not have to meet the top going rate to borrow the money needed due to the convertible provisions. Good grade bonds, convertible or not, do enjoy above average leverage possibilities, however.

While it might be fun to try, a book such as this can't explore all of the ways to invest in the stock market. The market offers a very wide range of investments and means for investing. Puts and calls, warrants, preferred stocks, selling short, etc., offer the knowledgeable investor many opportunities, a great variety of risk, returns, leverage and management. The main purpose of going into the market, as an individual, is to seek growth in stock, or fixed income through bonds.

Generally speaking, yields in the market are low, and since they have failed to keep up with inflation and offer no offset against income taxes imposed today on ordinary income, bonds aren't today's best investment. However, if you see hard times coming, bonds could be okay. Remember, it is the average wage earner who takes the biggest beating on taxes. Those with large amounts of cash or capital often can legally avoid the pain of the tax bite. The stock market is for the person not concerned with income taxes and who is satisfied with low yields, growth possibilities, and usually good liquidity. It is not designed, in most cases, for "keep money."

Risks in the market vary greatly from the new "penny" issue to the blue chips of great American industry and utilities. Some leverage is available, depending on the times. Management can be great or small, depending on what you invest in and how you invest. Every American who has accumulated some capital and has surplus dollars should consider the market. But you must find a good broker or be able to evaluate your investing as to risk, liquidity, management, inflation, yield and taxes accurately. Remember your goals, and most of all, remember real estate can offer anything the market can. Even more!

The purpose of the market is not to save your taxes or shelter ordinary income. Also, it will not give you immediate cash income sufficient to live on unless you have much capital to invest. It is possible to enjoy the advantages of real estate on less capital dollars than the stock market if you understand leverage and how it works. More will be said about this later in our discussion of group investment. The stock market is for possible growth, not income. It should never be used for income. It does have a good possibility of growth, but the beginning investor should always remember that the stock market is a speculation, and it is played by *speculators*.

Speculation means to seek a profit from market fluctuations. On the other hand, "crap shooting" means to seek a profit from "tossing" fluctuations.

We have an acquaintance in Michigan who has become famous as an investor in securities, primarily stocks. He has spent full time playing the market and has made a fortune at it.

Whenever he entertains in his beautiful home, one of his guests will invariably ask his advice on the market. To the point, they are looking for a tip on a sure thing.

He always replies by going to his wall safe and bringing forth a beautiful teak box, opening it before his guest, and taking out five gold-stemmed darts.

He then reaches into his safe and pulls out his portfolio of stocks, lays them in front of his guest for inspection and says, "These are my holdings in the market. They have all done exceedingly well for me."

"Choose any five you wish and I will make you a wager."

"I'll take this morning's edition of the *New York Times*—tear out the N.Y. Stock Exchange Sheet, hang it on this far wall, step off twenty paces and throw five darts at it. Whatever five stocks I hit, I will bet you they will do better in one year than any five stocks you choose of mine that have done so wonderfully for me in the past!"

Dart Williams never lost!

But then it must be pointed out that he was a good dart player!

Briefly, dabbling in the market is playing in the world's greatest legalized gambling game. The authoritative Gerald M. Loeb, in his wonderful book, *The Battle For Investment Survival,* said, "It is my contention that none of us knows what is going to happen to any stock, regardless of quality or history."

MORTGAGES   Score *23*

Mortgages come in a variety of risks and yields. High grade first mortgages are liens on real property, and usually have a fixed return of interest that is set at one to two points above the prime rate. Mortgages are nothing more than a loan to someone (or a corporation) secured by the borrower's signature and real estate. Most mortgages in the United States are loaned by savings and loan associations, life insurance companies, commercial banks, pension funds, trusts and sellers of property.

It is uncommon for private individuals to loan large sums of money in the first loan market, but it can be done by those with large amounts of cash and the time to wait for the full return of their capital. In today's market, mortgages are usually for a term of 20-35 years. Properly placed first mortgages are generally low-risk, low-management type of investments. As long as the mortgage is not over 75 per cent of the property's value, the only true risk to the lender is having to take the property through foreclosure, and inflation. The latter, inflation, has really hurt mortgage investors.

Remember, mortgages are a fixed rate yield. Therefore, your actual return must be calculated after income tax and inflation. The purpose for an investor going into the first mortgage market is to enjoy a steady yield with little involvement in management. Investors looking for growth, leverage, or income tax shelter, do not belong in first mortgage investments. They are hedges, however, against deflation.

Of course, there are other types of mortgages. The secondary mortgage market differs from the first mortgage market as to risk and yield. Many investors have made large sums of money buying seconds at discounts. Discounts can range anywhere from 10 per cent to 60 per cent. It takes very little math to see that by buying a second loan that was to yield 8 per cent, the yield to the investor would be 16 per cent, if the paper was bought at a 50 per cent discount. Many independent investors have involved themselves in the second loan market. The risk is usually much greater than the first loan market, but the yield and management is also greater. Anyone anticipating this type of investment needs to know much about credit lending, real estate values and titles. He should be backed by good legal and real estate counsel.

The purpose of this type of investment is to gain larger yields on capital. Again, the second mortgage lender must calculate his yield after inflation and income taxes. This lending is not one that offers tax shelter, growth, much leverage or liquidity to any great extent. But the second mortgage market does often offer a greater than average yield and a fixed rate of return. Each second mortgage should be analyzed individually as to risk.

A final word about mortgage lending—the seller of real estate who finds himself having to be a mortgage lender in order to sell is not in the same situation as the investor who goes into the mortgage lending market on purpose. There can be tax advantages and extra monetary gains to be made by offering the purchaser of a property better terms. In these cases, the seller of the property may find the purpose of the mortgage investment considerably different and much more purposeful than the average mortgage lender. Remember the purpose of mortgage investments. They offer little tax shelter, no growth or inflation hedge. They do offer good yields, low management and various degrees of risk.

ART, PRECIOUS STONES, ANTIQUES   Score 23

These fields can be rewarding to the investor. They take a high degree of management in their acquisition, care and marketing. The risk can be very great, but this depends on your skills of evaluating, selecting and marketing. Recently, rare books have enjoyed the greatest growth in value—even greater than stocks or real estate. You can become skillful in these items if you want to take the time to study and learn.

It is our opinion that any of these fields could become a profitable hobby for the average investor. But leave them as hobbies unless you want to devote much time to them. Enjoy what these items offer you in the way of enhancing your life with beauty. There is practically no leverage available in these fields. The risk of selecting them is as great as is the risk of holding them. Fire and theft are ever-present dangers. There is no yield, only fair liquidity and no tax advantages except capital gains provisions.

There are many more investments available offering less risk and management, more leverage and more tax benefits. If you must go into this type of field, get some expert advice. Learn everything you can on your own before you get into it. The purpose of this "investment field" is to occupy time and to receive pleasure from the holding of such items. A sidelight possibility might be the growth of capital. After all, if you finally do buy a great painting, are you sure you would want to sell it? Think about it.

THE COMMODITY MARKET   Score 27

The purpose of the commodity market is to make a market for the growers and users of produce and minerals. Speculators simply help them level out seasonal variances. To these speculators, the purpose is to enjoy quick gains on their investments by using as little of their own money as possible. The weather has more immediate effect on this speculation than does inflation because of the short term of time involved in the average commodity investment. Supply and demand are also very important.

Practically nothing in the way of investing offers any more leverage and appeal to the true gambler than the commodity market. But this field is not as complex as it seems. It's big. One entering the commodity for speculation stands to win Big and lose Big. It is a volatile and risky means of investing.

Management can be great if you can rely totally on your own judgment. There is no yield except in the final liquidation. Really good brokers in this field are scarce. Some account management companies have a good track record, especially those trend followers who also have common sense. This type of investing takes great skill, knowledge and Job's patience, plus the wise use of stops and guts.

Other than possible capital gains provisions, there is no tax shelter against ordinary income. Higher risk investments should be played with risk capital. To the average estate builder, to the investor with a definite goal in mind, to the person required to live on the yield of an investment, the commodity market has no purpose. To someone willing to gamble all or nearly all on getting rich without immediate regard to current financial safety, and who does not care about income taxes, the commodity market does have purpose. Playing the commodities is fun, active and exciting. But what is your purpose?

Now, that wasn't too bad. We were afraid we might say something bad about all of those other possible investments. Maybe you thought we would, too.

But, you'll agree, we did point out the good and bad points about those we mentioned. You've been exposed. Go poke your nose into any of them, but be a little careful with the ones we've warned you about.

In this book we've yelled at the banks and the savings and loan associations and the credit unions because *they* yell at everyone about what a wonderful investment in the future a savings account can be. We hope you have our position clearly in mind. We think savings is the place to keep your emergency fund money. And, well, er, that's about it. We don't think much of savings as an investment.

But the bankers know we're right. And, if you want to blame someone when you go down to lower your balance in your savings account to a sane level, tell the banker we sent you. Better yet, tell him that you're going to use some of your own money just as he's been using it ever since you opened the account. Tell him you are going to invest in American industry and real estate . . . because you want to see how it feels to be in the other 5 per cent. Be kind to him, however; you may want to borrow money from him.

There are so many opportunities for investment these days that making the decision is like trying to untie a double, wet knot in your gym shoes. That's what you're thinking isn't it? Well, we're about to launch into a discussion on insurance. What do you think of insurance as an investment? How much of that $158 billion in cash reserve insurance is yours?

We'll bet you a new pair of shoe strings for your sneakers that you'll modify your insurance after you've read Chapter 7.

CHAPTER 7

INSURANCE (UGH!)

Throughout the book we have pounded away at the importance of weighing possible investments, and we intend to show you why insurance isn't an investment or even a bargain. We will show you that it's an expensive necessity. When we've finished with that, we'll recommend one or two ways to buy insurance.

The various kinds of insurance policies available to us include term, ordinary, twenty-year pay endowment, endowment at age sixty-five, retirement income, president's special, founder's special, executive's special, the young man's special, the non-drinker's special, the nonsmoker's special, the housewife's special and the blue plate special.

There are at least twenty different kinds, including college plans, family plans and plans to cover everything. Very few life insurance agents understand all of them, and how can you be expected to understand them if he doesn't?

There are actually only two policies: term and endowment. Regardless of the compelling title on any of them, all of them fall into one of these two categories.

An endowment policy deals with two things. It deals with time and money. Both are variable, according to the policy. The time can vary and the amount paid by the company can vary. Let's put a face value on a policy, and let's examine it.

Assume the policy is an ordinary life policy with a $100,000 face value. It is a contract. The life insurance company is obligated to pay in the event of the policyholder's death if it occurs during the period of the policy. If death occurs either before or after the period of the contract, the company does not have to pay. Like life and death, every insurance policy has a beginning and an ending.

Let's say the face value of the policy is $100,000. It is an endowment policy, which means, specifically, that if you die before the contract is up, the company must pay your beneficiary. If you manage to live beyond the contract time, they, the company, will pay you the face amount. These are the conditions.

You must pay the premiums, and you must live for the policy to endow the face amount beyond the contract period.

A $100,000 policy for a guy at the age of thirty-five will have an average premium of $1,875 per year. Part of it goes to cash values so that by the time you reach fifty-five, there will be enough in cash values to pay you $54,000.

In the beginning we have 100 per cent pure insurance. If you die on the first day of the contract period, then the beneficiaries receive $100,000. Also, the day before the last day, it's the same. If you die the day before the last day of the contract period, then your beneficiaries will still receive only $100,000.

If you live to see the day after the end of the contract period, you can take the $100,000 out in cash value. The amount of pure insurance coverage goes from 100 per cent on the first day to nothing on the last day. At the end of the last day of the contract period, you no longer have insurance coverage with this policy. You have a cash value of $100,000. It's your money, you have thus insured yourself.

Every time you make a payment, you reduce the amount of insurance, and you build a cash reserve. Therefore, with an endowment policy of this kind, you cannot tell the guys at the gas station that you have $100,000 of life insurance after you make the first payment. You have a little less insurance and a little more cash value every time you make a payment.

The very purpose of the policy diminishes. You bought the policy for protection. That was insurance. Because you build cash reserves, the insurance part of the policy decreases. If you could take the part of the $1,875 premium that pays for insurance and use it to buy insurance, then you could take the remainder and put it in a savings account or securities or real estate. You would have the same sort of thing—insurance and cash reserve. And your beneficiaries would still get $100,000 if you died. That's how endowment insurance works.

The foregoing was the story of the "Insurance Financial Package." Let's compare this with a typical deposit term policy:

Age 35—Face Value $100,000—Premium $450 per year.

So now we find our first big difference. Each policy will pay the beneficiary $100,000 in cash on death during the life of the contract. But let's compare cost:

Ordinary Life Yearly Premium	$1,875
Deposit Term Yearly Premium	450
Yearly Difference	$1,425

That $1,425 difference is AT RISK!!!

Ten Years—$14,250. If you die your estate loses it. This is what the insurance companies claim is the Investment Feature.

Insurance has been included as a portion of this book for only one reason: the insurance companies have asked for it.

They are running rampant on television every twenty minutes between terrific action plays of our favorite Sunday football games, full-page ads in all the slick magazines, newspaper-planted stories, extolling all the virtues of life insurance as the "living financial package," the "acme" of the investment field. Only through insurance, they claim, can they do anything and everything to anybody and everybody. This, say they, is the prime investment of all.

So, inasmuch as this book is on investments in general and real estate in particular, we think we had best take up this subject of insurance as an investment, hold it up to the light and examine it accordingly.

When considering insurance as an investment, there are several important factors to look at. They tell us that the cost of a policy depends on (1) mortality, (2) the return on their investments and (3) expenses. But within these three areas are major factors which greatly influence the cost of the insurance: that is, the yearly premium that you and I must pay to keep our insurance in force. Let's look at these:

1. MORTALITY TABLES

The actuarial departments of the insurance companies predetermine with great accuracy when you and I are expected to die. And this is the foundation upon which all insurance contracts are based. A simple explanation of mortality tables would be the following: Of every 1,000 men in a given age group, each insured for $1,000, a certain number will die each year. Now the actuaries are able to predict with great reliability and accuracy, not who will die, but how many of the 1,000 will die. Every life insurance company uses a table of death and survival covering all ages from birth to 100. This is called the Mortality Table.

If ten thirty-five-year-olds were to die in a year, then the original 1,000 would have had to pay enough to give the beneficiaries of the ten who died $1,000 each.

But the insurance companies don't guess how many are going to die out of the 1,000; they know. They just look at their tables. Do you believe that these tables are adjusted every year so as to allow for all the latest medical innovations which prolong our lives? Huh! Guess again.

The first table in use was called the American Standard and was used from 1861 to 1948. The premiums on over one million policies still in force today are based on this particular Mortality Table of 1861, and the premiums are figured accordingly. This American Standard table was based on how many of the 1,000 men died during their thirty-fifth birthday year in the years *1843–1858*. This, if you can remember, was way back around the time of the Civil War, Lincoln, long before penicillin, transplants, modern medicine, Band-Aids and aspirin. The actual experience of the companies was that 8.95 of 1,000 men aged thirty-five died during the years *1843–1858*.

THIS TABLE WAS STILL IN USE 87 YEARS LATER IN 1948 AND THE PREMIUMS WERE STILL FIGURED ON THE DEATH RATE DURING THE CIVIL WAR DAYS!!!!!

Now let's look at the 1,000 thirty-five-year-olds. The group consisted of the sick, the lame, those ready to die, etc., and still only 8.95 out of the 1,000 died. So the table was set that the 1,000 would have to pay $8.95 each to guarantee the beneficiaries $8,950.

But are these the same people who were accepted for insurance? Hardly: that group of 1,000 would all have had to submit to a thorough physical examination, then a thorough check of their private lives and financial integrity. This should have eliminated a large percentage. So here we have them charging every one of the 1,000 a high mortality figure—but actually accepting only the "goodies." You ask what the actual mortality rate of those accepted was? In 1947, approximately 1.41 out of 1,000. This resulted in an overcharge of $7.54 per 1,000. This 1948 figure was changed, as the companies couldn't keep doing this. How long do you think you can hoodwink the public? Answer: 87 years! So the insurance companies changed the Mortality Table in 1948 to reflect the deaths in each age group during the years 1939–1940.

In the middle fifties, the insurance companies were gotten after: "Now, look, you're doing it again. Change your Mortality Table, we've had lots of improvements in medicine in the past twenty years, reflect it in your Mortality Tables!"

So they grudgingly gave in and set up the present table, which is known as Commissioners Standard Ordinary 1958. This went into effect in 1966 and is based on the American death rate for the years 1950–1954.

Let's see how these different Mortality Tables affect cost of insurance:

DEATHS PER THOUSAND

Age	Civil War Table	Commissioners 1941 Table	Commissioners 1951 Table	Actual Ins. Co. Exper. 1950
35	8.95	4.59	2.51	1.41

DEATHS PER THOUSAND—ALL AGES

1975 = 6.4%   1965 = 7.5%   1955 = 7.7%

Again, over one million policy owners are today still paying premiums based on Civil War mortality rates. Over seventeen million policies are based on 1941 tables and rates!

Say, hey! Have you noticed the ACTUAL mortality rate of the people they DO ensure? WOW!!!

The way the insurance companies "rig" their Actuarial Tables, there will always be an overcharge:

1. Mortality is figured on the sick, lame, dying, deadbeats, drunks, etc., within 1,000, but that is NOT whom they insure.
2. Mortality Tables are always figured from eight to eighty-seven years prior to putting them into effect. Thus, medicine gets better, our life expectancy increases—but it is years before we are given the benefit of this. Premiums are based upon the PAST, while death claims that are paid by the insurance companies are based upon the future.

Remember, the mortality figure is not supposed to allow for a margin of profit. Profit is ADDED later. Mortality is supposed to be PURE COST. Without any editorial comment from us, we thought you would get a kick out of the following statistics:

Year:	Average Age at Time of Death
1900	47.3
1940	62.9
1960	69.7
1970	70.9
1975	72.5

2. LAPSE

Lapse is the giving up, the surrendering of a policy due to:

    A. The inability to pay
    B. No longer a need

The average life of an insurance policy is seven years. Lapses, which are due in great part to "overselling," greatly affect the cost of insurance. In fact, 19.7 per cent of all policies are voluntarily terminated in less than two years after purchase.

For every chair you buy, you pay for the rejected ones; for every garment you buy, you also pay for the spoiled, rejected ones; the "goofs" add to the cost of the product you buy. This is equally true of life insurance.

The lapses are also actuarially figured and premium cost of everyone has the add-on factor figured in.

3. DIVIDENDS (or what makes the mutual companies so big, so rich, so strong)

First, the difference between a mutual insurance company and a stock company is primarily the issuance of dividends; or, to put it another way, the real difference between a stock company nonparticipating policy and a mutual participating policy is the price of the premium; OR, to put it as simply as possible, you pay more for a mutual participating policy than you do for a stock company nonparticipating policy.

A whole life nonparticipating policy, $100,000, costs approximately $1,875 a year. A mutual policy costs approximately $2,500 a year. Difference: the participating policy costs $625 more per year.

In the background we hear the bellow of the mutuals crying, " 'Tain't so! We let you participate in our profits—we give you dividends!"

What is a dividend? Ask any businessman or an IRS agent and he'll tell you, "It's a profit-income." That's true and, as such, is subject to a tax on that income.

Now we notice there are two uses of the word "dividend." The way you and I think of it as "profit," and the way it actually is in insurance, but falsely interpreted by them.

A dividend on an insurance policy is nothing but a return of an "overcharge" and, as such, is not taxable; it's your own money coming back to you—maybe!

Do you recall the difference in the premiums for the nonparticipating and the participating policies—$625? Well, you won't get that back the first year. Fifty per cent to 70 per cent of your total first year's premium went to the salesman's commission, so kiss your first year's overcharge good-bye. The second and third years, the companies are normally in a Cost Position, and you may or may not get a dividend (?) those years. In fact, you may or may not get a dividend (?) any year—and you will never know how much you may or may not get.

One company discovered that one of its agents had presented a prospect with a dividend illustration, the figures of which were 15 per cent above the company's own liberal estimate. When they called the agent to task for jacking up the dividend projection, he said:

> "What's wrong with what I did? You estimate dividends and feel that you're okay because you say clearly in the illustration, 'Dividends are estimates and as such not guaranteed.' Well, I say the very same thing in my illustration, too, only I think that with reduced mortality, rise in interest rates, etc., dividends will be 15 per cent higher during the next twenty years than what you expect them to be. *I've got as much right to guess as you have, haven't I?''*

In fact, by law, insurance companies cannot tell you that you will get a dividend (?) or how much it might be.

Did you ever wonder? If they are going to give the overcharge back, why take it in the first place? If you ask them, they'll tell you it's to be held in a reserve in case of a national calamity.

Then ask them how much they have in the reserve to take care of all policies AND THEN ask what is surplus, how much they have and what its purpose is and, last, what are "unassigned reserves." Boy, if you get this far with them, you will really be in for the greatest bit of double-talk your ears have ever had the misfortune to be exposed to.

Talk to your mutual man. As a mutual policyholder, you own part of the company and would like to know:

    A. Who makes the decisions?
    B. Who runs the company?
    C. How did they get their jobs?
    D. Can you vote?
    E. When? Where?
    F. Can you elect new directors?
    G. How are the directors chosen? By whom?
    H. Who elects the officers?

Then keep running!

4. COMMISSIONS

Did you believe the actual purpose of life insurance was to benefit widows and orphans? Look:

Actual Death Claims Paid in 1960	$1.5 BILLION
Commissions Paid in 1960	$1.6 BILLION

Now take a look at 1976—the insurance industry paid 21.3 per cent of their incomes to expenses and commissions, 9.7 per cent in death benefits and a grand .1 per cent to dividends.

COMMISSION SCHEDULES FOR SELLING:

Ordinary Life
Life Paid Up
Endowments:
  at sixty-five
  20 Year
  Life Income
	55 per cent to 80 per cent of the first year's premiums, plus a percentage of the next nine years' premiums.

Term Insurance	40 per cent to 60 per cent of the first year's premium ONLY

Naturally the premiums for all the cash value types of insurance above are approximately four times more than term insurance premiums!

So you can see why term insurance is not pushed. Which would you rather have as a salesman?

70 per cent of $1,875 = $1,312 Commission, PLUS!
- or
50 per cent of $450 = $225 Commission!

Overheard in an agency sales meeting:

"Now, men, from the above figures, you can see why you will go broke if you sell term insurance only. If you must sell term, use it as a door-opener so you can call back next year and convert them into one of our 'fat cat' cash value policies."

5. TWISTING

Replacement of an old policy with a new policy is called "twisting" by the agents who push "Permanent Cash Value" insurance, and it was meant primarily to stop an agent of one company from converting or replacing another company's policy. In insurance circles, this is known as "Laissez-faire."

    A. It is a "twisting" war where a whole life permanent policy is converted to term.

    B. Rarely is it considered "twisting" where a term policy is converted to a cash value policy.

You see, "Twist A" affects the income of the agent and the company, and it "smarts."

But "Twist B" helps their pockets, although it makes the policyholder "smart." So what?

Some claim "twisting" is misrepresentation. Did someone say, "By whom?"

6. NET COST

"Figures don't lie—but liars often figure," and, "There is nothing that can't be proved with figures," are two old sayings that have been applied by many people in many different walks of life.

Have you ever been asked this while being cornered in your favorite watering hole after an exhausting day at the factory:

> "Did you ever think you could own an insurance policy and it would COST YOU NOTHING? That your insurance coverage would actually be free? In fact, that you can make money on the deal?"

An eager or desperate insurance salesman has a well-practiced bit of numerical legerdemain that he resorts to when confronting a stalked applicant. To all the "pros" in the game, it is gleefully known as "Net Costing."

With but a few deft strokes of his poised pencil, he will quickly show you that your insurance doesn't cost—it pays—and that the premiums are not an expense but will be returned at a later date.

But, as we all know, all "tricks" are accomplished either with mirrors, by "hand quicker than the eye," or on assumptions.

Let's look at their numbers game of "Net Costing." First, the simple one used by those who sell nonparticipating policies. Here we go—ready?

A $10,000 Ordinary Life policy, annual premium $200, in force twenty years, with a cash value at that time of $3,000. At this stage of the act, the salesman will stop, lower pencil, raise eyebrow and shoot the following question: "How much did the insurance cost each year? Huh? Two hundred dollars per year? Naw!" he will say, "It only seems that way—watch!"

$200 × 20 years = $4,000 – Paid Premiums
Less – 3,000 – Cash Value at Time

$1,000 – "Net Cost" for 20 years

$1,000 ÷ 20 years = $50.00 per year
$50.00 per year for $10,000 insurance
or only $5.00 per $1,000

Before looking for the hitch, quickly sign the application. Pull out your checkbook, write the first year's premium of $5.00 as he showed above, and tell him he's got a deal. Let us know how you make out or tell us, "Which way did he go?!?"

Now on the real "pros" of the "Net Costing" racket—the "par" boys, those who sell dividends, the ones who take a big premium each year and then say they'll return it all in twenty-five years. Ready?

The Company's Way:

$100,000 Whole Life, age 40 to 100—Premium $2,800 yearly.

Total Premiums	$70,000
Total Cash	84,455*
Net Gain at 65	$14,455

*Includes cash values, dividends, plus termination dividends (based on 1969 scale), *guesstimated but not guaranteed for future years*.

Now let us look at this one closely. And here we find this "twister" has been accomplished by assumptions:

ASSUMPTION NO. 1:   You will keep the policy for twenty-five years.

FACT: The average life of an insurance policy is seven years.

ASSUMPTION NO. 2:   Dividends as shown will be paid during the next twenty-five years.

FACT: Can your banker tell you what interest rate he will charge for the next twenty-five years? Can your automobile dealer tell you what he will charge for your new car every two years for the next twenty-five years? Future dividends are nothing but "guesstimates" and should be accepted only as such. Remember, every agent or company has a perfect right to guess as much as they want. I guess.

ASSUMPTION NO. 3:   "The use of money has no value."

FACT: The insurance companies know the use of your (?) money has value—6 per cent when you borrow the cash value. (NOTE: Going up to 8 per cent shortly.)

The Factual Way:
Average Life of Policy—Seven Years

1.	Whole Life—Total Premiums @ $2,800	$19,600
2.	Term—Total Premiums @ $610	4,270
3.	Yearly Premium Difference—$2,190	15,330
4.	Interest compounded yearly on the difference	18,526
	Premiums plus loss of use of money (1+4)	38,126
	Less Cash Value, plus "guesstimated" dividends	11,536
	Actual Cost of Insurance (seven years)	$26,590
	Per Year	$ 3,799
	Per M	$ 38

Do you still want to talk about insurance as an investment?

We believe Mr. Harold J. Cummings, then president of Minnesota Mutual, put the nail in the coffin to this "twisting" act of

"Net Costing" when he addressed the American Life Convention in 1957. He said:

> "We may as well be blunt about it—any prospective customer must conclude that net costing comparisons, however plausible, are inclusive if not fictitious, deceptive if not deceitful, asinine if not downright dishonest."

7. LIQUIDITY

Almost all cash value policyholders are lulled into thinking that "their" emergency fund (cash value) is available whenever they need it. It is "their" money, being held for them by the insurance company. BE CAREFUL!!!

First of all, any money you have in cash value does not belong to YOU. You have no right, title or interest in it. It is owned solely by the insurance company and protected by the stewardship of the State Insurance Commissioner.

It's true you may BORROW it. If you do, you will have to pay the insurance company 5 per cent interest for using "their" money. Any time you have to pay someone interest for the use of something, you can bet it isn't yours!

There is another way you can get your eager hands on this money: CANCEL your policy! If you get the money this way, you then lose your insurance protection! You can't have both!

Lastly, they let you think this is your emergency fund. In time of need, it's there for you. Let's look at the record:

A national emergency: "The Depression." Remember how the banks had to close? They called a national holiday for *four days*. People had emergencies and couldn't withdraw their money.

As soon as this happened, the insurance companies jumped in and closed their windows on paying out cash values to the policyholders—not for four days but for SIX MONTHS!

One other difference: the banks closed both windows, paying and receiving. The insurance companies closed the paying window for six months but the receiving window was *never closed!*

Look at your policy and you'll see, in small print, that they may at any time take up to six months to lend or pay out the cash value. What did you say about an emergency fund? For a SMALL emergency it will probably be there. We guess.

In fact, all of the big insurance companies, at this writing of "Tight Money," are getting a bit uneasy due to the "run" on cash value borrowing. So much so, they are about to increase the 6 per cent interest you pay for using your (?) money in an emergency to 8 per cent.

Now let us look at the time when you do have an emergency and you wish to use the cash value you have built up:

Face Amount $100,000
Premium $2,800 per year
or $28 per $1,000
                    Cash Value $ 15,000

If you borrow the cash value, you will reduce the amount of insurance in force by that amount. Example:

You borrow the cash value of $15,000. You die the next week. Your widow will receive $85,000, not $100,000.

Let's continue this little investment (?) peanut game:

For borrowing the $15,000, you pay 6 per cent—$900—to the company. Then, at premium time, you pay the usual $2,800. That, plus the $900 interest, totals $3,700.

For how much insurance? Wrong! Not $100,000, but only $85,000. Now what is the price per thousand of your insurance coverage?

$$\$85,000/\$3,700 = \$43.52 \text{ per M}$$

and as long as you keep that borrowed money—your cash value (?)—the higher you pay for the insurance. Did you ever hear of that game, "gotcha"? They gotcha going and coming!

YOUR money?— — — HA! HA!

8. "FORCED SAVINGS"

One final argument given by the insurance agent: "peddling" cash value life insurance as an investment is the old chestnut about "forced savings."

They insist that the ONLY way most people can save is through life insurance. Further, that without the compulsion to pay life insurance premiums, thrift for the mass is unattainable.

Does the receipt of a premium notice in the mail at regular intervals make you thrifty? Was it the advent of life insurance that introduced thrift into your life? Our forefathers used to save prior to insurance and, in those days, they considered it necessary "hoarding."

What about the squirrels? Do you think the insurance companies taught them how to "hole it away"? The squirrels would probably chirp, "Aw, nuts!"

People save when and if they want to. Astute savers will reject life insurance as a real "loser."

Can you picture a policyholder who is subjected to the common disease within insurance circles of being "oversold," and this forcing him to save?

Strip insurance of all of the phony investment embellishments and you have a product that is fabulous, that can't be matched by anything else. Pure insurance has the ability to create an instant estate for a widow or an orphan. This is truly the miracle of life insurance.

Let's look at pure insurance. Pure insurance is protection insurance and, as such, can be very reasonable. Pure insurance is term insurance—and term insurance comes in two ways:

1. Level—meaning it has a level face amount for the life of the policy.
2. Decreasing—meaning the face amount of the policy decreases each year it is in force.

In both policies, there is little or no cash value.
Let's look at the difference in cost:

Ordinary Life, Non-Par (of course), Age 35 to Age 100, $100,000

Premium	$1,875 per year
Ten-Year Level Term (same as above)	610 per year
Yearly Difference	$1,265 per year

This $1,265 difference is at RISK! The moment the policyholder dies, this yearly difference is lost forever.

Decreasing Term, to 100	$ 450 per year
Yearly Difference	$1,425 per year

What does this premium difference mean to you?

$1,425 deposited in a bank for one year at 5 per cent would give you $1,425 Principal plus $71.25.
$1,425 invested in a good utility stock would return around $142.00—some good real estate may return even more!

If it is left in your Cash Value Life Insurance, you are only getting 2½ per cent or $35.62 return.

We make money only two ways in our lifetimes:

1. The money we earn by working.
2. The money our money earns for us.

Make *yours* work!

Insurance companies make us think our money has no worth, BUT money has worth and value when put wisely to PRODUCTIVE use!

There are various types of low cost pure protection available. If your insurance agent prefers not to show you the advantages and persists in "pushing" that old cash value investment stuff at you, keep looking for an agent who has your interests at heart.

Insurance as an investment (UGH)! Buy as much pure insurance for *protection* as you need.

Remember, the more you pay for life insurance, the less net protection you get, and the greater will be the loss of money to your estate if you die.

Well, we told you we were going to do a couple of things in this chapter about insurance. We've leveled with you about how we feel about insurance as an investment. It stinks!

But we didn't leave you nodding in agreement first and shaking your head in confusion later about what to do with your insurance. We have advised that you carry only term insurance if you're an investor.

Once you've freed up all of that money you've been wasting in insurance, what are you going to do with it? If you're smart, you're going to invest it in American industry and real estate.

If you go the stock market route, you're in for great ups and downs. If you go to real estate, why, friend, that's your best chance to get rich while you sleep!

CHAPTER 8

REAL ESTATE

There are few investment vehicles which offer the wide variety and range and possibilities of real estate. And within real estate there are individual investments with every degree of risk, management, yield, growth, predictability, liquidity and tax shelter.

Real estate offers every kind of investor the opportunity to reach his goals. The scope of real estate investment is fantastically broad. Real estate is as big as the whole wide world. In fact, that's what the world is. It's a great big piece of real estate.

Regardless of what your goals are, there is a parcel of this real estate . . . improved or unimproved property . . . which can be acquired to let you reach those goals. A man with only a thousand dollars down might find a lot or an older home to purchase. The land can be held for speculation, and the home can be held for income. On the other hand, a large corporation with millions to invest can use real estate as an investment or method of expansion. New cities will be built. Large tracts of land will be subdivided. Skyscrapers will tickle the clouds, and they will house businesses and families. Factories will be built for industry. And every single one of these requires the same basic element . . . real estate. Everyone interested in financial success can find it in real estate.

Sounds great, doesn't it? Well, that's exactly what it is. It's great. It's fantastic. It's unbelievable. It's wonderful, marvelous, fabulous, groovy, wild, swinging!

In order to understand the investment purposes of real estate, you need to understand the basic purpose of real estate.

We're right in the middle of the space age. But to get there we had to use real estate as the launch pad. No matter where we go, we'll need the land for support. We will need the land to stand on, and we'll need its products for our survival.

Everyone needs land. Our friends and neighbors around the globe are producing babies at a fantastic rate. That means more

81

and more people will be needing more and more land. The demand for land makes investors rub their hands together and smack their lips because of the great opportunities to make a whole bunch of money.

Real estate has the basic purpose of holding up a house or sprouting forth with things we can eat. Man uses the land to grow his food. That can be crops or livestock. Man puts his house on the land, his business on the land, his factories on the land, his water on the land, his fun on the land. And when he dies, he has himself placed into the land.

You just can't do anything without the land. No one can. Land, or real estate, offers the widest possible choices of investment, and for every popular item on the stock market, there is an equivalent in real estate. For example, investors might like highly rated, highly secured corporate bonds. They buy them for fixed return income, safety of capital, very good liquidity and little, if any, management.

The real estate equivalent would be property leased on a long-term basis to the government or a corporation with a high credit rating. At the other end of the line in the stock market are the highly speculative "penny" stocks. The equivalent in the real estate field would be inexpensive, highly speculative land off in the boondocks. And, of course, there's everything in between. Let's take a look at some of the types of real estate, and make some determinations about the basic purpose and the investment purpose of each.

Let's begin with something familiar. Everyone is familiar with a home, and almost everyone has some kind of a home. But let's talk about houses. The range is broad. Houses can cost from thirty to fifty thousand to some in the million dollar class. But the basic purpose of a house is to provide a place for people to establish a home or obtain shelter.

The home is the center of family activity. It's the base of operation. To an investor, a house can also offer a decent return if it is priced properly. The homes in the thirty- to fifty-thousand-dollar bracket seem to interest investors most. To a large majority of investors, a house is a way to get started in their real estate investment career.

A house can be obtained at a low down payment, it has a fairly high degree of capital security, and it doesn't require much management as far as the investment is concerned. If you bought it, then wanted to sell it, chances are good that someone else would be willing to buy it from you. That makes for an investment with good liquidity. Yield isn't too high, but you can usually plan on getting your money back plus a little extra when you sell it. A house is a great way to break into the investment field. It doesn't cost too much to get started, you can use it as a place to live while you own it, or hold it purely for investment. Since 1975, many areas of the country are reporting that houses have increased in value over 12 per cent per year.

Meanwhile, there's another kind of real estate investment called a ranch. A ranch has two basic purposes. One, it is used to accommodate livestock. Two, it usually has a place for a house. Even though the owner might be the operator, it doesn't have to work that way. Many large ranches are owned by individuals who never see them in action.

Generally speaking, however, the rancher invests his time and money into the operation of the ranch to make a return on his capital and labor. To the pure investor, the purpose of owning a ranch would be to have the opportunity of benefiting from the profit created by the livestock on the ranch. His direct income or direct profit would be from the livestock.

And those critters need the land, podner.

The management of the ranch can be either large or small, and this depends on the investor's ability to hire a caretaker or to be the caretaker.

If the ranch is priced properly, then it will have a fair degree of liquidity. If it happens to be located near an expanding city or a rural recreational area, the growth experienced in owning a ranch can be very substantial. But a ranch offers little predictability as to income. The elements of nature, the rise and fall of prices at the marketplace, and many other variable factors make it unpredictable on the income side of the fence. And, unless the ranch is located in an area of possible urban expansion, it can be considered as a high risk investment.

Yield is subject to all of those variables which affected the predictability, but in recent years many, many investors have gone into the ranching investment business because of tax shelters not always available in other types of investments.

Farms are like ranches, except that the income is from crops rather than livestock. And, like ranches, the investor can take an active or an inactive part in the management. Both require a great deal of specialized management.

The liquidity of a farm depends on its location, price and growth possibilities. And the growth itself depends on its location. Many farmers in the past have become wealthy by holding onto their land until the city needed it for its own expansion. An investor looking into the possibilities of investing in a farm should give extremely detailed consideration to the location of the farm he thinks he wants to buy. The growth of the investment may be entirely dependent on the location and the ultimate return on the investment.

Like the ranch, income isn't predictable, and investing in a farm can mean a high degree of risk. But in terms of long-term growth in the value of the land, income can be fairly predictable. That would mean that the risk would be reduced.

Yield from the farm can be small or great, of course. It depends on the crops and the management, the elements and the growth. But someone who needs income from the farm on a predictable basis shouldn't be too interested in a farm as an investment.

In summary, a farm produces an ordinary income and a swell way of life for the owner-operator if he has good crops and if the prices from the crops don't drop. To an investor, however, a farm investment probably means a small amount of ordinary income, possibilities of long-term growth in the value of the land, and some advantage of immediate tax shelter.

How about apartments? They come in all sizes from duplexes to multi-story high rises which make the skyline of the city more and more complex. The basic purpose of an apartment is shelter for people who need a place to hang the "there's no place like home" sign . . . without having to make a down payment. It is a way of life for many, many Americans.

There are apartment buildings to meet almost any investment requirement. A small investor just getting started can make a small down payment on a smaller unit, and, if he wants to, he can live there as the owner-manager. The large investor can invest in larger apartment properties, and management doesn't need to be a problem because larger apartments can afford professional management. The investor, in this case, is known as a passive owner.

Investment in the apartment field offers every degree of liquidity, growth, predictability, risk, yield, management and tax shelter. Right now large apartment complexes are very much in demand . . . by people who want to live in them and by people who want to invest in them.

Because apartments are either on short-term leases or on month-to-month rentals, the income stream can be changed periodically to meet rising costs and inflation. Factors like this add up to growth for the investor through an increase in the value of the property.

Apartments of all sizes have a great deal of predictability. As a matter of fact, sophisticated brokers are finding that it is highly feasible to run ten-year computer forecasts for projections on the income and expenses of an apartment building. This gives the owner or potential investor a long-term criterion on which to base his decisions.

Due to the fact that apartments of all shapes, sizes and descriptions are a basic commodity and necessary to house people, the degree of risk in apartment complexes is relatively low. Of course, there are always marginal situations, such as in an apartment house in a deteriorating neighborhood. This presents a great deal of risk to the investor. However, well-located, well-selected apartment buildings, coupled with good management, can make apartment house ownership a fairly *riskless* venture.

In comparing the general apartment house market to the particular kind of investment available through Wall Street, the apartment house is comparable to common stock. The greatest risk in apartment house ownership generally stems from management. Does the management understand the current rental market? Is it time to raise the rents or lower them? Are the expenses being held to a minimum? Is the property properly insured? Does it have the kind of financing on it, in proportion to the risk, yield and tax shelter, acceptable to the owner or owners? These are the questions that determine the risk in the ownership of an apartment house.

Generally speaking, the yield from apartments can be very attractive, ranging from 10 per cent to 30 per cent after income tax implications. The reason for this wide variance in yield is, again, directly related to management, location, growth, potential, the owner's income tax bracket, the age and condition of the building and area in which the property is located.

It is fairly safe to generalize that there is an apartment of some size for almost every type investor, that management can be what you want it to be. Liquidity is fairly good. Long-term growth is generally available. Predictability exists in an extremely high degree. Risk usually is controllable and much less than other type of investments. Yield is, as a rule, higher than other equivalent investments. *And* tax shelters in the apartment investment field can be quite attractive. Therefore, to the investor, the purpose of making an apartment building part of his portfolio is directly related to the kind of apartment that he selects. Nearly every investment purpose can be met in some type of apartment property.

In many growth areas of the country, apartment buildings are being sold at prices so high that there is no cash flow for the investor. Inflation is causing investors to buy now in hopes of later having cash yield due to rental increases. Many other investors are paying high premiums for converting apartment buildings to condominiums.

What about motels? The popularity of motels with the American public is now unquestioned. The basic purpose, of course, of the motel is to house people away from home. Motels offer shelter, food, recreation and meeting facilities. Again, there are all sizes, shapes and descriptions of motels. Some are operated by owners, others are managed by a professional team, hired and trained by a corporation whose specific purpose it is to own chains of motels.

The investment purpose of the motel is multiple. Depending on the size of the motel, it offers every degree of management. It can be a completely passive investment to the large motel owner who has hired professionals to run the operation.

The degree of liquidity available in motels varies because of size, location and the market situation. Usually, the best degree of liquidity is in larger motel complexes. Concerning growth, the motel can offer substantial rewards. Due to the fact that most motels are not on a long-term tenancy, the owner has the opportunity of adjusting his nightly rentals and incomes to keep pace with expenses and inflation. Just as in the case of the apartment house, this can add to the income stream of the motel, and it will be a growth type situation.

The motel is subject to many more economic factors than an apartment house. A change in the highway, area traveling conditions, competition, social or economic trends and accessibility give the motel a somewhat lesser degree of predictability than an apartment or office building investment. Large corporations have made a science of studying the predictability of the motel. They know that with continued good management and a well-selected site, the motel can be a predictable investment for as long as ten to fifteen years. In the case of smaller motels, not well located, the predictability is very low.

There is no doubt that the motel offers more risk than the average apartment complex. Although motels have less predictability and higher risk than some of the other media of investment in general real estate, they can offer substantially more yield. The yield, coupled with the risk, depends on many factors, mainly management and location.

Some of the income from motels can be from the restaurant-cocktail lounge and other activities. There are areas of danger within these activities because of the accountability of the funds and expenses connected with them. It can be summarized that the investment purpose of the motel is to obtain a higher yield and tax shelter, but the investor is going to have to accept the higher degree of risk and less predictability than available in some other realty investments.

The owners of most motels subject themselves to higher degrees of management than in the case of the apartment house, for example. But they can be well paid for this management. Some of the largest and newest corporations in America have been built on the principle of the motel. Motels offer lucrative rewards for those who understand the several elements of the industry and accept them for what they are.

Nearly everything that has been said about the motel is also true in the case of hotels. Hotels range in size from the small five- to fifteen-room hotel, bus-stop type operation in small towns, to giant, full-facility hotels located in large cities. Again, the purpose of the hotel is to house people that are away from home. Generally, management is not passive, but it can be. Liquidity is moderate. Growth can be negative or positive, mostly dependent upon management or location. Just as in the case of the motel, a hotel is not known for its great degree of predictability.

Think of all the services a hotel generally provides, such as food, beverages, room service, maid service, convention service, and on and on. Financial projections or analyses to determine the income and expenses of a hotel over a long period of time are most difficult. A hotel that is already in operation and proving itself has more predictability than one just built and yet to be proven.

There is a larger degree of risk in hotel ownership than in many of the other kinds of available real estate investment. This is largely due to the fact that hotels have to hire so darn many people. This causes complex accounting problems. On the happier side, yield from hotel ownership can be extremely attractive.

It is possible for the investor to own a hotel and lease it out to professional operators. This can reduce the ownership of hotels and motels down to passive investment with little or no management and a high degree of predictability. Most hotel owners are willing to accept a higher degree of management and risk, with less predictability, in order to obtain a higher yearly cash income or yield. Many tax shelters are available in hotel ownership.

Now let's talk about raw land. We have discussed the basic purposes of land, but what most people don't understand is that land generally goes through three cycles—user, speculator, developer. First, it is usually owned by a user. The user can be a farmer or rancher or a person who owns a building on the property which is providing shelter for his family or business. From this, the land goes into a speculator's cycle. This occurs when it is no longer feasible for the user to use the property in its present mode. Then, a developer often takes over and improves the condition of the ground or changes its use. It is then turned back into a user type of situation.

Generally speaking, the speculator slips in between the user and the developer cycles. The speculator wants to buy the property at a low price, and then hold it until it is purchased at a higher price and used by the developer. Let's look at an example of these three cycles.

Let's say a parcel of land is presently owned by a farmer. He is operating the farm to obtain his living. Everything may go along like this for years and years. Slowly, but steadily, the city grows out to the edge of his farm. A speculator sees an opportunity. He wants the property. He plans to hold it a few years and then sell it to a developer. He approaches the farmer and offers an option to purchase. Considering the speculator's offer, the farmer decides that the value of the property has increased to the point where it will be wise for him to sell to the speculator. He can take his cash, move further away from the city, purchase another farm, and enjoy the surplus benefits of the price he received over and above the pure value of the farm land he purchased farther out. A point comes when the value of the land has far surpassed its present utility.

Once the speculator obtains title to the farm, he might operate it to meet the expense requirements of holding the farm until it becomes attractive, ready and ripe for a developer to purchase it from him at a good price. This rewards the speculator for his holding period.

The developer then buys the raw land, and begins building on it. But he resells it to different kinds of users. It isn't farm land any longer.

This also happens with city property. Let's say a family has owned a small home well within the city limits for a long period of time. The character of the neighborhood has changed, and, like most of the other families, this family decides to move out to the suburbs.

A speculator steps in and purchases the home in hopes that some day he will be able to get the property rezoned and eventually interest a developer in building an apartment house. He holds the property until the population demands an apartment house. The land has a change of use.

At that point, a developer will become interested in redeveloping the property. He will purchase it from the speculator, tear down the old single family dwelling, and replace it with his shiny new apartment house. Once the new apartment house is built, the land returns to its original use as a dwelling site but on a different scale.

When you understand these three cycles, it's easy to understand the basic purpose of land. There is generally little or no management involved in land investments that have a moderate degree of liquidity, depending on price, terms and location. It has a very great rate of growth and predictability if it is well chosen, and it has a moderate to low risk. Land usually has no yield and it offers very little, if any, tax shelter. Therefore, the investor in raw land should look for two things . . . growth and ultimate yield.

Probably, more money has been made in land than in any other single type of real estate investment. Demands for land continue because of population and because man has found so many new ways to use the land. Growing affluence of the American population places great demand on the use of land as our recreational requirements, business and industries expand.

It isn't always possible to stand on a piece of land and project what value it will have or what demand may be present at the time a speculator wants to sell, and it does carry a greater degree of risk than the office building or apartment type investment.

One of the other great values for the investor in the ownership of land is extreme flexibility. Land may be subdivided, built upon, improved, rezoned, sold, exchanged, held, or leased. However, much of the future benefit of land speculation depends upon the owner's ability to retain the property until he can get the correct price. Most land speculators deem it necessary for the property to *double* in value in five years or less for them to make a profit on their speculation. This means that land must increase in value approximately 20 per cent per year. Because most speculators buy land with as little down payment as possible, they probably have carrying charges on the money they borrowed to purchase the land. This is an expense just like the other natural expenses of operation, management and taxes. It takes profit to cover them.

The chief goal of the land investor is growth. This means he has to buy the property at less than it will sell for some time in the near future. If the speculator has the financial capacity to retain the property as long as necessary, then there is very little risk in raw land ownership.

One word of caution about investing in land. Ultimately, land is only as valuable as what it can be used for. The trend throughout the country is to oppose development. Zoning regulations, the bush and bunny people, the no-growth folks who say, "I got mine, you go somewhere else," are taking their toll on raw land ownership. Be sure you know your opposition and zoning problems *before* you invest.

One of the most popular ways of increasing capital and enjoying returns from land today stems from land syndication. Land syndication enables an investor to scatter his funds in several parcels of land rather than just one.

What about office buildings? There are small neighborhood office buildings and, of course, huge gleaming glass and steel skyscrapers in any large city. Office space is just as necessary as apartments or homes. It houses people who are engaged in all sorts of business.

All the investment purposes outlined in our discussion of apartment buildings are usually present in office building ownership. The small investor can buy a small office building and manage it himself. By contributing his management abilities, he can enjoy a fairly moderate degree of liquidity, a chance for appreciation or growth, a fair amount of predictability, relatively low risk and high yield, and attractive tax shelter. To large corporations and syndicates, office building ownership can be strictly passive on management. It is more predictable than apartment building ownership.

With office space, the custom is to make longer term leases than normal to the apartment house field. Some offices are occupied by tenants who give three- to twenty-year leases, but the average is approximately five years.

Well-located office buildings with a moderate degree of risk can be compared to participating preferred stock. The tax shelter in office building ownership is not as great as it is in apartments, hotels and motels, but it does offer more tax shelter than equivalent investments in other investment classifications. Office buildings are extremely attractive to real estate investment trusts and large corporations. This has placed a substantial demand on the market for office buildings, and this raises the degree of liquidity. Most investors purchase an office building for immediate yield, growth and tax shelter. And it is interesting to note that there are many varieties of "office buildings." For example, a clinic is nothing but a specialized office building equipped for the needs of the dentist or the doctor. In recent years, it has become popular to put office space with warehouse space, and this gives the user a great deal of utility.

The future of all office space as an investment looks bright. Not only is business on a constant expansion, but also the amount of space each business needs is generally growing.

How about stores and shops? The basic purpose, of course, of stores and shops is to house retail and commercial business. To the owner-operator, the store or shop is merely shelter to house his business enterprise. However, to the investor, the basic purpose of the shop and store is yield, tax shelter, growth, predictability with little risk, moderate liquidity and a small or passive degree of management.

Shops and stores come in all shapes and sizes, from the single Mom-and-Pop neighborhood store to the sprawling, vast, neon-lighted shopping centers in the suburbs. A small neighborhood store or shopping center can be an attractive investment to the large corporation for syndication. Shops and stores offer every type of management situation. But usually it isn't as great in shops and stores as it is in apartment buildings, motels, hotels and smaller office buildings.

Well-located shops, stores and shopping centers offer a fairly substantial degree of liquidity and good prospects for long-term appreciation or growth. The predictability is very much along the same lines as is the office building, since shops and stores are generally put on five- to fifteen-year leases. Risk in shops and stores ranges from very high in small deteriorating neighborhoods to very little risk in large, well-established shopping centers. In comparing medium to large shopping centers with securities available through the stock market, shopping centers are similar to preferred participating stocks. By placing the tenants on long-term leases, the investor can be assured of a fairly constant and predictable income. Clauses in the lease for the owner or investor to participate in the income of the stores by percentage provisions are common. This means that after the tenant has reached a certain volume, he will pay a certain portion of his gross or net income to the owner. This is also similar to participating preferred stock, which usually has provisions for a certain predetermined dividend to be paid to the holder and at the same time a certain portion of the earnings of the corporation issuing the stock. Once this is understood, you can see how very comparable the participating preferred security is to the well-located, well-leased shopping center.

Yields available to the investor in shops and stores are very much equivalent to the yields available to the owner of an apartment building. Large shopping centers will yield returns comparable to a large apartment complex. Due to the fact that most shops and stores take such large parking areas, there is not as much tax shelter available in the shop and store area of real estate as there is in the home, farm, ranch, apartment, motel and hotel or office building types of investment. Because the investor cannot depreciate anything but improvement, it is easy to see that a shop or store requiring much parking ground will substantially reduce the size of the improvement. This means less available depreciation for the investor.

There are several classifications of shopping centers. Regional shopping centers can cover forty or more acres. They can attract 125,000 to 275,000 customers, and usually there is an anchor tenant, such as a large department store. In some cases, there are two large quality tenants. The smaller shops huddle about them like little chicks. Next there is the community shopping center, usually on twenty-five to forty acres. These are designed to appeal to 5,000 families or more in the immediate area. As a rule, the major tenant will be a supermarket or a junior department or variety store. Shopping centers appealing to approximately 1,000 families, covering ten acres or less, are called neighborhood centers. The primary tenants are supermarkets, drugstores and service type tenants, such as barber shops, beauty shops, clothing stores, etc. The future for the small, neighborhood strip store generally does not look too good. The rapid advance of the regional and community shopping centers seems to be putting a great deal of burden on the smaller complexes. However, there are many individual situations that completely alter this statement.

At the present, the greatest future in the store and shop field is in the large community or regional shopping center. The risk is almost completely dependent upon the location and competition in the area.

Like warehouses? The basic purpose of the warehouse is to house industrial and commercial processing storage activities. There are all kinds of warehouses, from the highly specialized, such as those offering refrigeration or dust-proof storage, to common, ordinary, everyday warehouses we see filled with products and goods manufactured by industry. To the owner-user, the warehouse is merely shelter for his business or products. To the investor, the warehouse is generally sought as a highly predictable, low management type investment.

Individual warehouses or warehouse complexes are usually leased to business and industry for ten to twenty-five years. The average probably is somewhere between fifteen and twenty-nine years. This gives the owner-investor a passive management situation with a good, constant and predictable yield. In most cases the yield on this type of investment is lower than is the case of apartments. But it depends on the credit rating of the tenant. Risk is very slight as long as the property is leased and it is in direct proportion to the demand for warehouse space and the credit stability of the tenant. Warehouses offer an average amount of tax shelter and fairly good liquidity, in comparison to other real estate investments. Because of the fact that most warehouses are leased to tenants on long-term basis, they have become attractive to estate trusts, pension funds, profit-sharing trusts and corporate investors. They know what their yield will be without involving a great deal of their time and management. Comparing the warehouse to a security available in the stock market area, we would say that a warehouse compares to a bond, possibly a convertible bond. We know that the bond will have a constant yield over the years as does the long-term leased warehouse. However, the convertible aspect is this: At the end of the lease the owner stands to renegotiate the lease at a higher price, thus adding to the value of the income stream from the property.

Generally speaking, the investor will purchase a warehouse when he is not too concerned with the growth or a high rate of tax shelter, but is interested in a lower, yet substantially predictable yield.

How about the factory? By and large, factories are owned by the industry or corporation requiring them for manufacturing. There are many cases, however, of factories being owned by investors and leased to the enterprise requiring such a facility. In this case, the purpose of the investment is predictable yield with a low risk, a varying degree of tax shelter, passive management, good liquidity and low to moderate growth. Factories, like anything else, come in all shapes and sizes. They can be large plants, like a steel mill, or very small neighborhood factories manufacturing dog food.

Very small manufacturing firms, in most cases, do not have high credit ratings. Therefore, they can offer a high to moderate risk. Factories leased to well-known multi-million dollar corporations offer little or no risk as long as the lease runs. Factories owned by investors are generally leased to enterprises on longer term than warehouses. They can offer more predictability and less chance for growth due to inflation. Of course, the leases can be written with an escalator clause which provides that the tenant pays more rent in direct proportion to, let's say, the cost of living index. This should be considered in analyzing any and all leased properties.

The first step in evaluating the investment potential of a leased property or any other type of income property is to take a close look at the quantity and quality of the income. The quantity, of course, has to do with the yield on the formulas we have given you, and the quality has to do with the strength of the tenant signing the lease.

What about recreational and resort real estate? Resort properties, such as hotels, hunting lodges and boarding facilities, generally involve a high degree of management. The liquidity, of course, is dependent upon size, location and income stream, and growth can be an erratic situation which depends on the whims of the public.

At one time a very profitable property to own was a bowling alley. As social trends made bowling slightly less popular, many bowling alleys were thrown out on the market at prices showing substantial losses to their owners. These situations cause negative growth. On the other hand, the booming ski, racquetball, and tennis facilities are enjoying extremely rapid growth, and they are showing substantial appreciations for the owners.

Resort and recreational real estate investments have less predictability than many of the other types of investments within real estate. This can be caused by the elements, social trends, cast obsolescence and, of course, management. Risk in most recreational type property is greater than in basic types of properties used to house people, business and industry. It has often been said that yield is in direct proportion to risk. If the risk for these facilities is higher, so is the yield. Tax shelters can be moderate to high.

The basic investment purpose of recreational and resort property is high yield, directly proportionate to management responsibility. Of course, it is possible to own some type of sport facility that can be leased out to professional managers. In that case, it would become the purpose of the investment to yield its owners a small return with more predictable income and passive management.

You can compare resort and recreational property with new issues on the stock market or corporations with less than blue chip or Triple A credit ratings. There will be more fluctuation in the profit potential of these facilities. But with the growing affluence of the American public, there is plenty of money to be made in resort and recreational properties in the future. This being the case, investors willing to accept the higher risk stand to reap the rewards of substantial appreciation.

Looking over this brief examination of the purposes and types of investments available in real estate, it can be seen easily that there is great variety. We have had to generalize because there are so many, many kinds of properties and degrees of financial situations that it is virtually impossible to give the investment purpose of each and every different type of property that could be placed in an investor's portfolio.

In summary, it can be said that properties not subject to long-term leases offer the greatest appeal to the investor in the form of moderate risk, great predictability, moderate management, moderate liquidity, moderate to high yield, substantial tax shelters and high growth. On the other side of the coin is the long-term lease property which offers a very high degree of predictability, low to moderate risk, low to moderate yield, low to moderate tax shelter, low to moderate growth and an average degree of liquidity. Management ranges from completely passive to moderately passive.

People who are knowledgeable in the field of real estate investing often chuckle when they hear someone say, "I'm going to invest in corporate bonds to get a safe, predictable yield. And I'm not concerned about growth and tax shelters." They often give these as reasons for not going into real estate.

That's why it is so important to point out all the various types of real estate available to you. What could be more predictable than a twenty-year lease to a blue chip corporation? The lease will yield more than most tax bonds, it will have more predictability, less risk, just as much liquidity, more chance for growth, passive management, and much more tax shelter. And everyone is interested in saving taxes. Between a twenty-year lease and a corporate bond, which is the safest type of investment? Would it be a bond issued by DuPont, General Motors, etc., or a twenty-year lease on property occupied by a blue chip corporation? Real estate can offer you more security than the above bonds and give you 50 per cent more income with a twenty-year lease on the General Motors building on 59th Street in New York City. If GM leases that building from you for twenty years, they will pay approximately 7½ per cent to 8 per cent. Now, would you rather have that bond of GM's or hold the lease on their building? Just a thought. If they couldn't pay their lease, they absolutely could not pay their bond. That is why it is so important to know all the possibilities available in this dynamic field of real estate. Aren't you glad we told you?

CHAPTER 9

LAND

It was also said many years ago by a Colonel Oswald that, "An acre of ground can't run away, it can't burn up or down, it can't be stolen or hidden away out of sight. It represents the most solid, substantial and permanent investment possible. Most of the great historic fortunes are based on land. Land does not explode, farms are not carried away by panic, trusts cannot get a corner on the earth and yet it is the source of all wealth."

Probably no other single commodity in the next fifteen to thirty years will enjoy any more rapid growth and demand than raw land. Nearly everyone stands to profit from the acquisition, holding, development and resale of that old stuff we call *terra firma*. The land speculator, the lot hustler, the farmer, the investor, the participant in group investments, the mighty corporation. Wall Street, the real estate broker, the stockbroker, the pessimist and the optimist . . . all stand to benefit from the increase in population that will put unceasing demands upon the land. Some statistics from the U.S. Bureau of the Census may provide guidance for land investors. Between 1960 and 1970, population percentage increases in the fastest growing states were: Nevada—up 71.3%, Alaska—up 33.6%, Arizona—up 36.1%, California—up 27%, Colorado—up 25.8%, Florida—up 37.1%, Maryland—up 26.5%, and New Hampshire—up 21.5%. Look for this trend to continue, especially in the Sun Belt states where less fuel is needed to keep warm. These percentages, which have nothing to do with numbers of people, are examples of what gains many of the states can expect. Over the next ten years almost every state will see an increased influx of population. Hook that up with an increase in income, and you'll see fantastic opportunities to use and profit from land. Nearly all living creatures, or creatures created by law such as corporations, gobble up land at unprecedented rates.

Look at many of the western states. Everyone says there is so much land available, how can it possibly increase in value? These

lands are held, to a large extent, by the United States government. Large reserves are set aside for national forests, parks,
monuments, highways and superhighways, Indian reservations
and game preserves. On top of this, you can add local municipalities and state governments, which also own vast amounts of
land not available to private enterprise or individuals for immediate use.

There are 365,482,000 acres of land in Alaska. Only 829,000
acres are not owned by the United States Government. Here is a
brief rundown on some other western states and the government's land position.

STATE	TOTAL ACREAGE	NOT OWNED BY FEDERAL GOVERNMENT
California	100,207,000	55,588,000
Colorado	66,486,000	42,520,000
Hawaii	4,106,000	3,851,000
Idaho	52,933,000	18,817,000
Montana	93,271,000	65,625,000
Nevada	70,264,000	9,691,000
New Mexico	77,766,000	51,092,000
Oregon	61,599,000	29,468,000
Utah	52,697,000	17,241,000
Wyoming	62,343,000	32,302,000

These are just a few examples of the amount of land in many
states owned by the federal government. Rather than decreasing,
these figures will climb. Military reservations and highways, of
course, account for a great deal of the continual acquisition of
land by various governmental agencies. What does all this mean?
It means that the great expansion going on in the west is going to
be limited by governmental needs and controls. Therefore, pri-
vately held land is much more scarce than we think.

Who has made big money in land? Many of the names in
American history books we read as kids in school, including
Henry Ford, Andrew Carnegie, Marshall Field, John D. Rock-
efeller and J. P. Morgan, made large percentages of their vast
fortunes in land. You don't have to be astute or particularly wise
to realize that land is a fixed commodity, and that population
increases will make a continually growing need for more land.
This demand creates values. And an increase in value means
someone is going to make a profit. Industrial giants, presidents of
the United States, governors, ranchers, janitors and factory

workers have acquired moderate to great wealth through land ownership.

While the average man sits around his living room in the evening, being bombarded by the propaganda put out by Wall Street through the TV tube and newspapers, others are out making sure bets in land acquisition investments. Of course, there are people who have invested in land and have lost. But most economists will tell you that if the owner of land has the financial capacity to retain his ownership, ultimately he will benefit financially. Now, most of us don't want to wait forever or supply our great-grandchildren with adequate income because of sacrificial land purchases we make today. This can be avoided by understanding the growing population boom and shift that is coming in the United States, and by wise selection of lands that are available to us now. Listen to this story about a businessman in Georgia.

He and nine of his friends decided to get together to form a stock investment club. Each contributed $100 a month. This happened in 1957. Because none of the businessmen studied or knew the intimate details of the stock market, they called on a large Wall Street brokerage firm which had an office in Atlanta. The Atlanta office was more than happy to send a representative down to the small town to guide the newly formed investment club through the maze known as the stock market.

After monthly meetings for nearly 10 years, and a combined cash contribution of nearly $120,000, the businessman leader of the group asked the stockbroker to give him an accounting of their success over the ten-year investing fling. The Georgia businessman, who didn't know too much about real estate, decided this was a fantastically low return for all the effort, cash investment and meetings over the years. With a red face and a pounding fist, he told the stock peddler to return to Atlanta, and to completely liquidate the investment club's portfolio. Then he went to a real estate broker and told the broker he had approximately $140,000. He wanted to make a real estate investment that would show them some real action, and he didn't want another ten years to go by with such low return.

The broker located 300 acres of land on the outskirts of a small city where it was a well-known fact that a major interstate highway would soon be constructed. The land was priced at around $450,000. The highway would cause population expansion in the small town and it looked like the price was okay.

The irate investor gathered his club together, told them his ideas, and proceeded to talk them into placing the $140,000 down on the property. The seller was going to carry a mortgage for the difference. In approximately twenty-six months the interstate highway rights were acquired by the government. Within a few days, the word was out, and oil companies were knocking on the doors of the investors to acquire rights on the corner of a cloverleaf intersection that was going to be constructed on their ground. Within six months, they had sold enough filling station sites to retrieve their initial down payment completely. A while later, a major motel chain came in. They purchased a five-acre site adjacent to one of the oil company sites. The $110,000 they received from the sale of the motel site went to reduce the mortgage.

A short time thereafter, a small manufacturing firm moved from Ohio to Georgia, and acquired a twenty-acre site which completely cleared the mortgage. So, with only twenty-nine acres of ground, plus what they had received from the federal government in the condemnation of their land for the highway, they were able to liquidate their mortgage. That left 270 acres, free and clear, and they had inquiries from developers and speculators. By 1973, all land was sold and their ultimate net profit was $800,000.

This is not an unusual example. It happens every day to people who are willing to take calculated risks in land investment.

The average worker drives through some parcel of land every day that will increase in value terrifically. Probably it is obtainable for extremely low down payments. There have been land investment opportunities in every town, city and hamlet across the nation. Twenty years ago a machinist working at the CF & I Steel Corporation plant in Pueblo, Colorado, was offered what is now the fabulous ski slopes of Aspen, Colorado, for $2.00 an acre. Today, it has value up in the millions. When he was asked why he didn't buy it, he said $2.00 an acre was too much to pay for ground that could only graze sheep.

Everyone has heard of the fantastic success story of increases in value in southern California, Florida and Arizona. But there are opportunities in everyone's own back yard. Land that was plentiful twenty years ago in the mountains is now in demand by those people who can afford summer or recreational homes or ski slope condominiums. Raw desert land is being converted into cities in the sun for the retired, and even the "Watts" sections in the center of our large urban areas are in demand for new development.

There are many success stories in land, and we'd like to tell you one about a widow in North Dakota. When her husband died, he left her $10,000 in an insurance policy. She realized that $10,000 wouldn't go very far and that she wouldn't be able to feed her three children very long on what was left after the expenses of the funeral. She went to the outskirts of her small city, and she purchased ten acres of ground with a small house on it at the intersection of two old country roads for $15,000. Friends and relatives tried to talk her out of buying the land because she would have a mortgage of $5,000 on it. She had in mind that the family could keep a cow and grow most of the vegetables they needed. It would help her keep the food bill down.

At the same time, she took in sewing from the neighbors, raised chickens and sold eggs. Her family did miscellaneous chores for the neighboring farmers, and in this manner they managed to get by. Finally, her daughter got married and her two boys went off to college. They worked their way through the University of North Dakota.

Almost twenty years after she bought the property, a developer approached her, and he offered her $205,000 for the property. It seems as though the two old country roads had become major thoroughfares and the city had grown out to her small family farm. There were even smart suburban homes beyond her in the country. The same $205,000, now properly invested, gives her a safe retirement income, far surpassing anything that can possibly be produced by "socialistic security."

HOW HAS MONEY BEEN MADE IN LAND?

Land Values Double in Last Decade

Industry figures show that in the last ten years, land values in the United States have doubled in most areas.

As a result, all kinds of land investments—in commercial lots, city lots, farm land and resort and recreational area property— have proved to be extremely profitable.

Since 1967, the price increase in common stocks as measured by the popular stock indicators and excluding dividends has averaged approximately 7.84 per cent. On the other hand, land prices in the same period, since 1970, have shown an estimated 200 per cent increase.

This tremendous increase in land value is one of the reasons for the higher costs being experienced now in home and construction costs.

Even though we appear to be experiencing something of an economic slowdown, land prices are expected to continue rising. As one expert explained, "Land is one item whose supply just

can't be increased. As more and more people move to the cities
and as they demand more roads and recreational facilities, land
values and prices will inevitably rise.''

The Federal Housing Administration has announced that the
average price of home sites carrying FHA-insured mortgages has
risen from $4,300 in 1970 to $15,000 today.

Not only is the general public being hit by skyrocketing land
prices; even Uncle Sam has felt this rise. The National Park
Service has to pay twice as much today as it did a decade ago for
National Park land. Federal highways are costing 175 per cent
more in land acquisition than in 1960.

All of the above indicates that land investment today will
possibly provide better returns to the investor than it did ten or
fifteen years ago. Land that is well-situated in the path of progress
will definitely provide a better investment than that which is
located out of the mainstream of the tremendous growth being
experienced in the United States today.

Probably one of the most flexible of all investments is raw land.
There are so many things that can be done with raw land to
benefit the owner that they are almost too numerous to list.
Basically, land can be used in thousands of different ways.
Agriculture is only one use. Land can be subdivided, rezoned and
exchanged, developed, leased, syndicated, held for appreciation,
or simply retained to use as collateral for loans at the bank. Let's
take each of these methods for making money in land and see why
they have proved so profitable to the raw land investor.

The Subdivision. Probably one of the best known methods of
creating large sums of money out of raw land investment is the
subdivision. It is a well-known fact that you can buy almost any
commodity cheaper in larger parcels. Wholesale mercantile companies apply this principle when they buy a carload of flour, and
then resell the flour to various markets in smaller amounts.

For centuries, man has been buying large parcels of ground and
subdividing. It's not uncommon to buy twenty acres of ground for
around $200,000. After putting in roads or streets, and possibly
some utilities on the land, let's say there are only sixteen one-acre
sites left for resale. To the man who wants an acre site, $40,000 is
not an unreasonable price. Assuming that each acre costs $10,000,
and that improvements cost $10,000 per acre, there is a potential
gross profit of $20,000 for each of the remaining sixteen acres.

If the owner is in a position to expend his capital and wait until
all the lots are sold, he will have all of the capital back plus a
profit, before taxes, of $20,000. More often than not, this repre-

sents twice his original down payment. He can use the newly acquired capital to purchase a larger parcel and repeat the same procedures.

Grand scale subdividing has attracted big money, big corporations, and even some big crooks. As a result, local, state, and federal governmental agencies are producing regulations faster than General Motors is making cars. One of the most significant requirements on subdividers these days is imposed by HUD. This governmental agency now requires all subdividers to file a HUD REPORT, which must be sent to anyone interested in buying a lot. What the prospectus is to the stock business, the HUD report is to subdivisions being sold across state lines. Attorneys charge around $100,000, or more, to create these reports—obviously interstate site selling is reserved for the big boys in today's climate.

Like anything else, subdividing is much more complicated than it was ten years ago. It is very risky for amateurs—if you are feeling drawn to this still lucrative aspect of real estate, be sure you hire a knowledgeable real estate consultant to take you through your first venture.

Rezoning. Rezoning has to do with changing the legal use of the land. Most municipalities have passed zoning ordinances which require properties to be developed in certain ways, and the use is restricted by the zoning code. Areas or neighborhoods that are changing in characteristics very often lend themselves to future change in zonings. Of course, everyone has heard about the influential investor and the crooked politician who team up to create higher values in land through influence and political manipulations. Although this may be the quick way to bring about rapid changes in zoning, it is abhorred by the honest landowner and honest land speculator. It is not necessary to be a crook or a political hack to get rezoning. Most planning commissions or zoning boards are receptive to ideas which will provide legitimate development progress, and they are willing to change zoning maps, if it can be proved that the change will benefit the community. These are the things you should think out well in advance if you plan to purchase property and later rezone it.

Land Exchanges. One of the most fruitful methods of realizing a profit in land is to exchange it. Exchanging, when properly handled, can be accomplished tax-deferred which is sometimes referred to as "tax-free." Let's look at an example.

There is a dentist in Chicago who purchased eighty acres of

land for an investment next to one of the booming suburban areas, just west of the city. He paid $100,000 for the land and in just five years he was offered $225,000. If he accepted the $125,000 profit, he would be subjecting himself to capital gains taxes amounting to about $35,000. Of course, even after taxes, he would have had a substantial return on his investment. But, because he was fortunate enough to have a knowledgeable investment real estate broker, he exchanged the property for a small office building in another Chicago suburb.

Due to the fact that he accepted no cash in the transaction, and then acquired a property with a larger mortgage on it than the property he gave up, he made a completely tax-deferred exchange. This meant that the $35,000 which would have gone to the government was now working for him in the equity of the office building.

Section 1031 of the Internal Revenue Code allows the tax-free exchange of property providing it is being held for production of income or being held in a trade or business to be exchanged for any like property without being penalized with income taxes. The definition of *like* for *like* property is simply this: You may exchange any property that you are holding for investment or business purposes. Contrary to some of the bad advice being put out by accountants and attorneys who haven't read the tax code, this method has provided many millions of dollars in tax savings for the wise and astute investor. It simply means that you can take a piece of raw land and exchange it for an apartment house, a shopping center, an office building, a warehouse, or even another piece of land. If you want the exchange to be completely tax-deferred, you must not receive any cash or boot or net mortgage relief in the transaction.

Development. We have already touched on development as one of the possibilities for making a good return from raw land ownership. Let's say that you purchased a piece of raw land and you have held it to a point of development or redevelopment for a new user. Even though the land has increased substantially in value, there is the possibility that you might develop an office building or an apartment building on the property and retain it for income without having to pay any tax on the increase in the value of the land because, in effect, you have not sold the property.

Many professional builders and developers warehouse land for this precise purpose. In other words, they go beyond the path of immediate development, purchase land, and place it in their inventory until they are ready to use it. In this manner, they are acquiring property at lower prices, converting it later to higher and better situations.

Developing can be an extremely complex and risky enterprise for the novice. Even some well-known, highly skilled developers have taken a financial bath when they inadequately estimated the higher and better uses for the raw land. On the other hand, there have been many amateurs coming into the field of developing who have taken raw land and made substantial gains on their investment by producing a development that has great user appeal.

Development, to the land speculator, is this. He will put his property to new and higher productive use without suffering the consequences of income taxes for the appreciation he has enjoyed in his holding period. There is a possibility of taking unproductive raw land and changing it into income property by developing an income property facility on the land. He stands to substantially increase the price of his land because he has found a new use for the property. Providing that the project is successful, he can increase his profit via the development route. By putting some type of improved property on the redeveloped or vacant land, he can create a new income situation, and he benefits from the ownership in tax shelters.

Lease. Raw land lends itself well to lease situations. One of the most dramatic stories of profitability in land speculation via the lease method happened in a large midwestern town. The speculator bought a seemingly low, swampy property that was generally used as a grass and trash dump by the surrounding neighbors. After holding thirty acres for nearly fifteen years, he finally obtained rezoning by promising the city he would clean up the eyesore, level out the land and put it into productive use as a shopping center.

Although the man was not a developer, he knew that there were many commercial tenants who would lease the land from him to build their own improvements according to a professionally prepared plan for a shopping center. His original cost of acquisition was around 10¢ a square foot, which adds up to about $4,300 per acre. Now he is leasing some of the land based on a value of $35 per square foot. Most land leases of commercial nature will command an 8–12 per cent return. For every square foot of land he leases at the rate of 10 per cent he gets $3.50 a year return on an original investment of 10¢. It takes no mathematical genius to multiply this times thirty acres to see what fabulous income this land speculator has built for himself by the lease method. On top of all this, because he has not divested himself of the ownership of the land, he has not subjected himself to any capital gains increase because of the fabulous appreciation of the land. He has created new utility, he has created a facility that the neighborhood very much welcomes and, at the same time, he has transformed a swamp into a large successful investment. Now he rakes the money in every month.

In recent years, the development of the franchise business has caused a sharp increase in the demand for leased commercial sites. Franchise companies do not wish to invest their capital in real estate because they need their funds to expand and to operate their businesses. This makes an ideal situation for a land speculator to acquire a piece of raw land and lease it later to a company with decent or blue chip credit in order to obtain income from the raw land. Oil companies have been doing this for years. This situation also creates a combination of the land lease and the element aspects for the land speculator. Countless business institutions across the country that will lease land ask you to construct the building for them. Then they lease it as a total package at a rate sufficient to make it profitable for the land speculator who builds or has the building constructed to put the land into productive use. The same trend is popular now with the industrial user who leases warehouses, and the land under them, for factories, airport sites, ski slopes, recreational facilities, office buildings, condominiums, and, yes, even homesites. Much of the land in downtown Manhattan and in Miami Beach has not changed ownership for generations. Yet, new projects replace buildings that haven't stood long enough to become obsolete. This change of use of the land has been made available by land-lease situations.

Again, we have to caution you about long-term leases that do not provide for a cost of living increase on an annual basis. If your net land lease doesn't keep up with inflation, it will act contrary to the normal increase in value. In other words, your property value will decrease.

Group Investing (Syndication). We already pointed out in the case of raw land that the investor in a position of buying larger parcels of unimproved property is in the best position to reap greater rewards. One of the great disadvantages of land ownership is that it is usually purchased on low down payments. This creates a mortgage on the property which requires a *cash* outgo to meet the payments and taxes on the property. Although it is to the advantage of the investor to use leverage or other people's money in the acquisition of these properties, it can become a great financial burden to have to make payments on property which does not produce any income. This situation has discouraged most small investors from participation in highly profitable land speculations.

An extremely popular method for the moderate to small investor to enjoy the rapid growth and appreciation in land is to use "syndication." Syndications or group investments, whichever you prefer to call them, allow many people to get together, pool their money for the down payment, and share proportionately in the mortgage payments and holding expenses. There are situations all over the United States where ten to fifty people with common goals have entered into agreements with each other to pool their funds in order to hold their property until it can be developed, leased or resold profitably. This makes the burden on each investor lighter. At the same time, it gives each the potential otherwise available only to the investor with large sums of money.

Later on we will be going into group investments in more detail, but it is essential to point out here that just because you don't have large sums of money or large amounts of ordinary income to make high mortgage payments, it doesn't mean that you have to avoid land speculation as an investment.

Probably the most common reason values can be obtained in the ownership of raw land is "appreciation." Appreciation is caused by several factors, such as population increase, change of use, and increase in the types of uses to which land can be put. This is the plain and simple example of an investor who buys a piece of property, and holds it until some willing soul comes along and pays a higher price than the investor has expended to acquire and hold the property.

In order to be successful at this game you must be a good buyer. You have to be able to go out and see a piece of land, and then have enough confidence and enough foresight to predict accurately that the value of the property will increase. Surprisingly enough, it is not as difficult as it may sound, as there are many astute professionals in most communities who can assist you in your original land acquisition.

Also you must be a good seller. This means that you should know the proper time to sell. And you should know how to price it. You must know what terms to offer on the property, and also you must know when the property has reached its peak value in your hand. Again, the assistance of a professional is extremely valuable, and the advice can be obtained at a low cost. Land investing is great, but put a professional on your team.

Look around you. Has your neighborhood picture changed at all in the last few years? You might have an opportunity right in your own back yard. Buildings are going up all around us. That

means less and less vacant land. If there is less land available . . .
and more is wanted . . . then the price must go up.

"Underneath all is the land."

Arthur Brisbane said it, more than twenty-five years ago,
"Governments rise and fall. Fashions and values and paper
securities do likewise. But land remains." He also said, "After
you have your home, buy other Real Estate for investment, profit
and future independence. Except in Real Estate ownership, time
works against us. Time makes us old, time puts everything out of
date . . . diminishes all values except in Real Estate. For yourself
now, for your children in the future, buy good Real Estate."

WHY REAL ESTATE VALUES WILL GROW

1. Highway development will continue to be a powerful factor
in the growth of real estate values.

2. The automobile industry: Highways give us the traffic and
then all highway services must be built—motels, service stations,
drive-ins, and shopping centers are needed to take care of the
traffic.

3. Leisure time: We have more and more time to enjoy ourselves. Golf courses, amusement parks, bowling alleys, the
"freedom" lands, the Disneylands, resort lands . . . all need land.
And that spells REAL ESTATE.

4. Retirement: People are retiring at earlier ages, and they are
moving to warmer climates—Florida, California, and the South-
west.

5. Population explosion: It took all of our years as a nation for
our population to reach two hundred million. It is estimated that it
will take only thirty more years to double that population.

6. The diminishing supply of land: Real estate feeds on itself. In
turn, this causes higher values for the remaining and yet undeveloped portions of land.

7. Energy shortages will increase the demand for redeveloped
inner city properties—expect a move back to the core city.

8. Environmental concerns and governmental regulations are
making it more difficult to develop land and new structures.
Expect these pressures to drive up the prices of already-to-be
developed land and existing buildings. High cost of mortgage
money is also fanning this fire.

9. The lack of utility availabilities, water, gas, sewer, and other
services, are making existing properties with services accelerate
at historical rates, yet they may very well remain today's best
buys.

HOW TO OPERATE IN LAND

Speculate—The Other Way to Develop. The speculator tries to buy in the path of development, and he holds until he finds someone who will give him a profit on it. The developer, on the other hand, usually buys the land for a specific use. He improves it, and then either sells it for a profit or holds it for income. To speculate or develop intelligently takes more than buying land on the outskirts of a city and waiting for the population to spread out and create an added value so that your land can be sold at a profit for development. Most people tend to operate in land on a haphazard basis. When they do, they stand to lose because of excess estimates on the future value of outlying land and over-optimism on the possibilities of development. Even when a city spreads out to embrace outlying land, a fair portion of the available land is bypassed. Premature land subdivision and haphazard development account for this.

RAW LAND

Undeveloped acreage offers the greatest profit potential. This is because it can be bought at the lowest price, and it offers the possibility of selling at the highest use. Raw acreage is any land which is not in use and for which no specific use has yet been determined. In selecting raw acreage, we will be interested primarily in the location and in the character of the land itself. If it's hard, dry and flat, it will command a premium price. If it's low and wet, or if it has steep slopes, it will have to be marked down to accommodate the cost of making it usable. The major pitfall in buying acreage is that you might buy it too soon at too high a price. On the positive side, you have several factors going for you when you buy raw acreage:

1. The push of population against a limited supply of land.
2. Leverage.
3. Taxable deductions such as interest, tax payments, etc.
4. Profit will be realized at a capital gains tax rate.
5. A hedge against inflation. The opportunity for diversification by buying several small plots.
6. Split-off—the chance for selling some of the property at the original purchase price and still having a great deal of the land left.

BASIC RULES TO FOLLOW IN BUYING ACREAGE

1. Is the land a good buy? The factors which relate to this answer include judgment as to the potential of the land, its current market value, its quality and its probable future use.

2. Patience and wherewithal. Are you prepared to hold this land for the necessary investment period? No set timetable for investment in raw acreage can be established, but since even the fastest growing population moves to suburban areas slowly, you should plan to hold on to raw acreage for at least five to ten years. But remember, a 100 per cent increase in value with a 30 per cent down payment is actually a 333 per cent profit.

3. Check and double-check the availability of utilities, zoning, and access before you buy. Also, take a good look at your potential competition.

LEVERAGE ON RAW LAND

Raw land can be bought for such low down payments as 5 per cent to 15 per cent equity, and the major portion of the investment represents tax deductible interest payments on a purchased money mortgage with no personal liability. Leverage produces higher net gains than with equivalent gains in the stock market.

COMMERCIAL LAND

There are many ways to speculate in land for commercial use. Commercial values tend to grow with residential development. When you buy a large tract of land, anticipating future residential development, the road frontage can offer future commercial values. Also, there are many risks. For example, many people buy vacant land zoned for commercial use, looking for future capital gain. But they are disappointed because the land is already overpriced, because somebody else nearby jumps in with more resources and develops another piece of land to meet all the immediate commercial needs for the community. It pays to be fast . . . and right.

INDUSTRIAL LAND

The best places to buy land for possible industrial use are on the outskirts of rapidly growing centers and in rural areas which are being brought closer to the city by new freeways. There are several ways to speculate in industrial land.

1. Buy raw land suitably zoned and located for future industrial use. This is speculation on a rise in the value of land located suitably for industry with respect to highway, rails, source of labor supply, etc.

2. Acquire land for industrial use and develop it as a planned industrial park.

RECREATIONAL LAND

One of the biggest economic developments in America is the increase in leisure time. This is coupled with the increased number of retirees with pension money to spend and a growing high school and college population with more spending money from more prosperous and indulgent parents. It all adds up to more boating, golfing, bowling, skiing, swimming and all sorts of fun. Part of your fun could be in owning the land where some of the action happens.

LAND FINANCING

Carry-back mortgages by the seller are the most common source of financing the purchase of land. This is because the seller is in the best position to take back a mortgage, and he can get a better price and tax advantages for his land by doing so. Owners are the largest source of financing in the country.

OPPORTUNITIES IN LAND INVESTMENT

What other salesman can say this about his product?

1. It is limited in quantity as to the amount available for sale.
2. It is an item of which no more quantities will be manufactured in the future.
3. It is guaranteed never to wear out.
4. It is not adversely affected by inflation.
5. It may be used in a multitude of different ways.
6. It will be increased in demand for years to come as population increases and the need for living quarters and supporting areas increases.
7. It is almost certain to become more valuable as time goes on.

Compare that to different types of investments such as Savings and Loan Deposits, stocks and bonds. As you know, one of the important factors is the annual return that may be anticipated

from the investment. Here are some representative average returns on these investments:

Government Bonds	5% to 6%
Savings and Loan	5% to 10.5%
Preferred Stocks	6% to 8%
Common Stocks	4.5% average
Utility Stocks	7% to 11%
Mortgages	9% to 12%
Improved Real Estate	5% to 20%
Acreage	15% to 100%

Other factors of importance to investors are the security of the
investment and the liquidity. In terms of security, the first four
items listed would probably rank in that order, assuming that the
stocks are in listed companies. As to liquidity, these same four
are types of investments which can be converted to cash readily,
assuming again that the stocks are listed.

And we agree that investment in real estate cannot compare
with the other types of investment insofar as liquidity is concerned. It should not be considered by people to whom this is an
important factor. As to security, real estate would undoubtedly
rank below investment in Government Bonds and Savings and
Loan Associations. However, it should compare quite favorably
with investment in stocks on this point.

The principal question then is what kind of return may be
anticipated from these various types of investments. It's easy to
determine the return from the history of the average return on
groups of common stocks in the past.

1. All of the purchase price is applicable to land, which is the
item carrying the appreciation potential.

2. When buying acreage in large quantities you have a built-in
increased value by a mere division of the property. A thousand-
acre parcel can be purchased much more cheaply than a hundred
acres, and the thousand-acre parcel can always be pieced off to
purchasers of ten-acre parcels at a much higher price.

3. Undoubtedly, raw acreage will continue to increase more in
value as a result of the population increase and new land-use
requirements.

Well-located acreage that will double in five to seven years can
easily be found by the knowledgeable real estate investment
counselor. It's a strange thing—we hear many, many stories of

how people have made big gains in land, but we have heard very few stories of people who have lost money. Is this fact or fancy? It's a darn fancy fact.

It was Grover Cleveland who told us, "No investment on earth is so safe, so sure, so certain to enrich its owners as undeveloped realty. I always advise my friends to place their savings in realty near some growing city, there is no such savings bank anywhere."

CHAPTER 10

INCOME PROPERTY

As far as the definition is concerned, income property means some type of real estate that is meant to produce income for the owner. The income can be derived in two basic ways. One, the property can be leased to someone else, and the owner is the passive investor. Two, the property can be nonleased, which means the income will be more flexible and possibly a little less predictable.

Generally speaking, it is pension funds, profit-sharing trusts, banks, investment trusts, and corporations that seem to have a hang-up for leased property. These people seem more concerned with being able to have a high degree of predictability for their beneficiaries or investors. On the other hand, investors looking for situations from income properties that allow growth, keeping pace with inflation and generally a higher return, are more interested in the nonleased property. There are many variations to these classifications—for instance, three-year leases as opposed to ninety-nine-year leases, and apartment buildings on month-to-month tenancy as compared to the resort hotel operation.

What is generally important for the investor to understand when considering the purchase of income property is how to analyze the income stream. The old saying could be put this way: "Income is not necessarily income."

Several years ago in California some real estate brokers decided to climb out of the doldrums of ignorance by getting more advanced education in the field of income property and the analysis of investment. The movement was called the Certified Property Exchangers. It was to be a designation that would recognize those who had made intensive study in the field of income property analysis, exchanging, investments and taxation.

The CPE theory was simple. There are three kinds of income. Taxable income. Net spendable income. Net equity income. The theory went on to say that it was absolutely necessary to analyze the property from every standpoint and to analyze the property *and* the owner or prospective owner together with these types of income. The discoverers of this theory worked hard and long at the monumental task of educating fellow Realtors in the theory. They designed forms and formulas to aid those less creative and academically astute than themselves. The process went something like this. First, the broker went into the field. He found a property and began to collect all the data necessary to perform the mathematical calculations and gyrations needed to determine the three types of income. He checked the age and size of the structure, the type and quality of construction, the type of neighborhood the property was in, and all the other physical aspects of the property that had been done in previous years by any astute real estate broker and/or appraiser. At the same time, he took the time to understand all the income ramifications. He determined what the gross rent was, he developed an accurate expense picture, and he analyzed the owner's books, if possible.

He did everything possible to check the fair market value of the rentable space, and then he went on a little further. His next step was to determine the useful life of the property so that he could begin to understand the income tax aspects of ownership. At this point most real estate brokers would get the listing signed, rush back to their office, put an ad in the newspaper and hope the telephone would ring. He would wait for someone to come along who could afford to buy the property. But not the Certified Property Exchanger.

He was taught to go home, sit down with all the facts that he had gathered in the field, and begin to apply all these numbers to a form. This form is called the Property Analysis. First, he determined the owner's present position, and then he made another property analysis on the way he thought the property should be run. Then he projected a property analysis on what kind of financial circumstances the new owner would most probably experience by buying the property. He considered leverage, financing and terms. After the various property analyses were completed, he went on to complete a form called a Comparison or Projection.

Most of the figures in this comparison or projection are based on a net operating income, and the idea of trying to determine the three types of income was simply this. What looks like income may very well not be income unless you consider your secret partner, Uncle Sam. To calculate taxable income, it is necessary to subtract from the determined net operating income, or that income left over from the operation of the property after all expenses had been paid, any interest payments on a loan, plus the depreciation. The depreciation schedule, in accordance with government regulations, has to be figured out accurately and, because interest payments are deductible, these two items are subtracted from net operating income. This results in taxable income.

To a person in a high bracket, a negative taxable income can be a very desirable thing. It simply means that you can take the tax loss and apply it to your other ordinary income, reducing your overall tax liability.

It is necessary that you understand the *theory*. Without the basic understanding of this three-income approach to the analysis of income property, you are not going to be able to determine whether a potential investment income property is going to be beneficial to you. It does no good to say that any investment gives you a $1,000 a year yield or a 10 per cent yield if you are talking about yield before income tax. The important money is "keep money."

"Keep money" means the amount of income you have from an investment that is truthfully yours to keep after all tax liabilities have been paid. When someone walks up to you and says they have invested in a stock that is now yielding them 20 per cent, a good question for you to ask is, "20 per cent before tax or 20 per cent after tax?" One of the most dramatic examples of income tax implications can be applied to the common, ordinary, everyday savings account. Let's consider a man in a 50 per cent income tax bracket who has invested $10,000 in a savings certificate that yields 9 per cent. Without the use of an IBM computer, you can tell that his first year's earnings will be approximately $900. However, because interest income is taxable, the government would take half of that income, and he'd have $450. His yield, then, has not been 9 per cent. It's 4.5 per cent. And we haven't even considered what inflation did to the purchase power of the $10,000 certificate.

This same theory can be applied to income property. If you should own an income property that actually gives you tax shelter, in other words, protects some of your other income from the tax collector, you should give credit where credit is due. Let's assume a property brings in $1,000 and actually reduces your tax bill another $200. In reality, that property has earned $1,200 for you. Since the only thing we are concerned about is how much we are earning on the actual amount of money we have invested in the property, we can express that $1,200 in a percentage of our equity investment. Therefore, this resounding theory about the analysis of investment property dictates that you subtract any tax liability from the income of the investment or add to the normal income any tax savings you might have. By following these simple steps, you are able to arrive at net spendable income.

Net spendable income simply means the amount of cash you can put in your pocket. In order to determine this on a piece of mortgaged income property, we take the net operating income as above defined and subtract from it the principal and interest payments on the mortgage. Professionals call this answer "gross spendable income." To this gross spendable income figure, either add or subtract the income tax implications. Let's say that our gross spendable income is $1,000. Also, let's say that we are in a 25 per cent income tax bracket and the property has saved us $250 in tax savings. We would determine that our net spendable income is $1,250. On the other hand, if the property did not give us a tax shelter, and we had to pay $250 to the income tax collector because of the income from this building, we would say that our net spendable income is actually $750.

Now you can see two of the important types of income streams that we have from an investment of any kind. We only have one other important type of income to determine so we can fully understand the benefits or lack of benefits an investment can give us. It's called "net equity income."

This simply means we take the net spendable income and add to it any growth the property enjoyed, expressed in dollars and cents, plus any reduction that may have occurred in indebtedness, such as a mortgage. Let's consider a simple example. Let's say our net spendable income is $1,000. Over the course of the year we reduced the mortgage $150. Now we would have $1,150 worth of benefits from the property. At the same time, let's say the value of the property had increased $500. By adding all of these together, we would arrive at the fact that our net equity income was, in fact, $1,650. Now, of course, all of these figures can be expressed in percentages of the original down payment. That's adding frosting on the cake so that we can compare our percentages to other similar investments or any other investments in our portfolio to see what the end result is in an actual percentage figure.

What happened to the average real estate broker who tried out for CPE? Fewer than 30 per cent of them passed the course. As the years went along, other great minds entered the field and added even more sophistication to this method of property analysis. Because of real estate's great predictability, they were able to project these figures over five, ten, fifteen, even twenty years with a very reasonable degree of accuracy. The calculations were long and tedious, and were therefore generally avoided by the average real estate broker.

Eventually the Certified Property Exchanger's program was taken over by the Realtors National Marketing Institute (RNMI) (Commercial and Investment Division). They built a solid faculty of knowledgeable members from around the United States who could teach this to their fellow brokers. The program is now called "Certified Commercial Investment Member" (CCIM).

In between all these steps we have outlined here are many other complicated steps that actually won't do you any good to learn unless you're in the business. It takes years of experience and many, many hours of high-level instruction to be able to understand it. The important thing for you to know is that when you seek the purchase of an investment of any kind you should seek qualified professional help. If the broker you are talking with doesn't understand everything, then move on down the road and find someone who does. Generally speaking, the CCIM's, of which there are less than 700 across the United States, are about the only people you can really count on to know these facts.

Because the above calculations are so laborious, someone finally got the bright idea of having computers do all the work on these calculations. (See the example of computer printout on page 124.) These calculations are based on professional analysis and judgment and carried out by the mathematical computations of the computer. You will find now that knowledgeable real estate brokers and investment counselors across the United States are using the big magic black box to project taxable income, net spendable income and net equity income, among other calculations, over a period of ten years on computer printouts. What used to take the best investment counselor, or CCIM, eight hours or more to calculate, the big magic box can do in approximately four seconds. It takes fifteen minutes to complete a beautifully printed statement for the investor to eyeball.

What a beautiful system it is. For the first time, it's possible to analyze an owner, together with his income tax situations and financial structure, and apply the data to the ownership of a property. It's the only way to understand the income of any type of investment property. To show you how sophisticated this procedure has become, it's possible to take a negative net spendable income situation from land, but add a predicted rate of growth, and know how you will come out according to these three highly esteemed income approaches to an investment property. The idea that you must actually join the owner and the property together with their financial circumstances is so important that it can mean the difference between profit and loss.

A typical example might go like this. Let's say there are two absolutely identical apartment houses built side by side. They have the same income and same expenses. They are made out of the same color brick, were built by the same builder and have the same quality management. They are identical twins, financially and physically.

Along comes Mr. Gotrocks. He buys apartment building No. 1. Because of his high income tax bracket, he can enjoy a substantial profit from the ownership of the property. The property next door can be bought by an investor in a very low income tax bracket, and he can just barely break even or possibly show a loss on his investment. Understanding all these theories and actually practicing them is like trying to fill your own cavities. Leave the cavities to the dentist, and leave the analysis and projection of income property to the expert.

These fabulous new computer printouts can show you how long a period you can expect to enjoy the income from a property without paying income taxes. They can compare the yield from an income property, after taxes, to what you would have to have in yield from a non-real estate type investment in order to enjoy the same kind of income after taxes. They even project how much income tax you will have to pay if you ever sell the property in any one given year. On top of that, they'll tell you how much income tax you can save if you make a completely tax-deferred or tax-free exchange on your holdings.

The professional investment counselor, or knowledgeable real estate broker, always gets a kick out of an owner who says he has owned his property for ten years and is still getting a 50 per cent return. Because of the way depreciation is calculated, property decreases over the years. Most owners don't realize that the longer they hold their property, the more likely they are to be losing some of the benefits they could have on a new property or an original property. As the various medical organizations advise, everyone should have a yearly checkup. This is also true for income property owners. The benefits of ownership usually decrease over the years, and having a professional analysis done on a yearly basis is the only way to tell when the benefits have decreased to the point where it would pay to exchange for another property or sell the existing ownership and purchase a new one.

Take a look at your own investment portfolio. You will have to calculate the three income approaches as you've learned them here and you will probably find you are not obtaining the yield you thought you were. The financial analysis and the understanding of income tax implications is much more important than many of the more popular items that investors and would-be investors think about when they are about to purchase a property. For example, it really makes no difference whether the building is made of blond brick or red brick, has a high-pitched roof or a low-pitched roof. Brick-kickers would be shocked out of their minds if they knew that the beautifully well-constructed building they recently purchased had about half the actual after-tax yield as the junk their local broker showed them that almost made them gag. Now this is not to say that the quality of construction or the location of a new property is not important. It is. But, we are saying that so many people are so busy looking at the putty in the windows, the filters in the furnace and the scratches on the doorcases that they overlook the most important aspect of income property—the income stream as you now know it from the above income approach theory.

It is also a funny, yet sad, situation when a potential buyer of an investment or income property thinks that he doesn't give a damn about the income tax implications. He just wants to know what the "true" income picture is. He proceeds to get out a sharp pencil, cut down the existing income, and add in more expenses. He arrives at a figure capitalized at the proverbial 10 per cent net income, and then he shoots the owner an offer based on his un-astute calculation. There have even been cases recorded by knowledgeable real estate brokers that have made it possible for people in higher income tax brackets to buy absolutely vacant buildings and show a better yield on their invested dollar than they could have had if they'd had some of the so-called glamor issues peddled by the boys in button-down collars and pinstripe suits on Wall Street. Even the highly regarded appraisers' profession has not yet come around to understanding that it is financial engineering that can make or break an investment property. By this we mean leverage.

Income property, as it applies to real estate, generally enjoys a high leverage factor. In other words, you can borrow a lot of somebody else's money to buy the joint. Let's take an example of what leverage or O.P.M.—Other People's Money—can mean to the investor. Take a $10,000 house (We know there aren't any decent $10,000 houses. This is for example only.) and say that you bought it free and clear as a rental property. Say it produces $100 a month real income. At the end of the year, you will have earned $1,200 gross. Now, because this is pretty cheap rent, let's say that you as the owner are only responsible for paying the taxes and insurance and some maintenance which adds up to about $500 a year. You have earned a net operating income of $700. This represents a 7 per cent return, before taxes, on your $10,000 investment.

Now, without considering income taxes, let's go to the same situation where you bought the same $10,000 house on $1,000 down and had the owner or bank carry-back the other $9,000. If you end up with the same $700 before debt service and income tax implications, everything looks the same. However, let's also say that you paid $720 interest on the $9,000 loan. It looks like a $20 loss. However, remember that you have been paying off some of the loan. Let's say that adds up to another $200 a year. Subtracting the apparent $20 loss from the $200 equity buildup, you can see that you made actually $180 on your original investment of $1,000. That's 18 per cent. That is 11 per cent more than you made in the case where you bought the property on a free and clear basis. Probably no other investment in the United States today offers any more opportunity for the small investor to use O.P.M. than does the investment in income real estate. These factors can apply to a small house or to a gigantic skyscraper.

If you will turn to page 124, you will see an example of a five-year computer printout as used by the many CCIM's. The actual printout can run for one to twenty years. However, as you will note, only five years will be illustrated due to limitation of page size.

BUY LOW–SELL HIGH THEORY SHOT DOWN

There have been lots of rumors going around that the only thing you have to do to make a profit in business is to buy something at a low price and sell it at a higher price. This, says the old adage, makes the business world go around, and it is absolutely necessary if you are going to obtain financial success. A full knowledge of income property kills this old wives' tale. In the ownership of income property it is still possible to make money even though you sell for a lower price than you originally paid for the property. Here is an example.

Let's say that ten years ago you purchased an apartment house for $100,000. You placed $25,000 down in cash and obtained $75,000 in a loan at 7 per cent for a period of twenty years. Over the course of the ten years you held this property, you have been amortizing or paying off the loan systematically. Now the ten years have passed. You resell the apartment building, but you sell it for a $10,000 apparent loss. In other words, the selling price is $90,000. At the time, the loan balance will be paid down to $48,200 and the cash you receive from the sale is $41,800. You have increased your original amount of down payment 67 per cent. In other words, you had $25,000 when you went into the property and you had $41,800 when you came out of the property, even though you had sold the property for $10,000 less than your original purchase price. Income taxes have not been taken into account.

Also, there have been other possible benefits. You have taken some cash out of the property over those ten years, for sure. You have had some income tax shelters, but we are not even counting those here. This proves in dollars and cents that you can buy a property at fair market value on a leverage situation, and some time in the future you can resell it at a lower price and still benefit from the ownership of income property. There is definitely a time to buy and a time to sell income property.

Analyzing each situation, not on the price you paid but on benefits you had during the course of ownership, is the only criterion you should use in determining whether or not to sell. The vital thing to remember in the above demonstration is that it is the tenants who have been paying off your loan. That didn't have to come out of your pocket and you, therefore, stand to make a profit even though it looks like you have sold the property at a loss.

From the above illustration you should also be able to see just how little risk there is in the ownership of income properties. In fact, the risk of not owning income property is far greater than the chances you take in acquiring title to some suitable income-producing property. There are investors and would-be investors, investment advisers and so on, who preach constantly that real estate income property ownership is a very risky situation. When you buy a share of stock, even on margin, who pays off the indebtedness? The corporation in which you bought the stock? Through dividends? Ha! Ha! The average dividend paid by companies listed on the New York Stock Exchange in 1977 was 4.62

per cent. How the devil can you pay off a margin loan on a stock if you are paying 8–10 per cent interest to the bank when the average stock only yields this small dividend return?

Of course, there are people around who remember high vacancy rates in apartments, empty warehouses, abandoned shops and stores. This is a fact in business. There *is* competition in the income property field, and there are cycles when we have an overabundance of available improved properties to house people, commerce and industry. Even then, in many cases, income property can and does make its own way. That means paying expenses and reducing indebtedness. That reduction of indebtedness is actually income. Besides, since you understand that you don't have to buy low and sell high, you can see that the possibilities of your making a good return in income property, even though it has had marginal occupancy, are extremely good.

Let's also compare the ownership of income property to that of the systematic purchase plan of mutual funds. In this plan, you contract to buy so many dollars worth of mutual fund shares for a prearranged period, regardless of the price of the stock. In this case, you, of course, intend to come up with money out of your pocket. Every month you cough it up to make the investment. Therefore, it is your pocket money and your ordinary income that is building the equity in that particular mutual fund. This is not necessarily true with income property, however. Once it is purchased, and you can manage the property properly, you can expect *tenants* to reduce the indebtedness on your property. Other investment advisers say you had better not get into income property because it takes such high management.

Later on we are going to have more to say about the management of income properties; but from having read thus far, you now know there are various kinds of income property. Just exactly how much management do you have on a warehouse leased to an AAA concern for a period of twenty years? The answer to this is that you probably will have to go to the mailbox each and every month to collect your check. That kind of management can be handled by almost anyone. There is an income property for every management capability and desire. There is an income property for almost everyone, regardless of his original capital investment. Take for an example the well-read William Nickerson, author of "How I Turned $1,000 Into A Million In Real Estate In My Spare Time." To the sophisticated professional real estate investment counselor of today, Mr. Nickerson may be an amateur. He was successful because he understood the principles of income property. It makes no difference if you have to start out by buying cheap, run-down little houses. As long as you have the desire and the talent to rejuvenate the property, you stand to make a profit and benefit from having your dollars working for you.

You can see that you don't have to sit around studying every classified ad that comes out in the newspaper, or search your area over from stem to stern in order to find a bargain in income property that assures you success. More often than not, you can buy a property at fair market value. With the advice of an expert in the income property field you can attain a position in income property that will yield you twice as much as the other highly advertised and more common type of investments. Don't wait. Find a good real estate investment counselor or knowledgeable real estate broker. Let him sit down with you to determine where your assets are and how much money you can put into income property. Let him help you determine your goals, and then let him proceed to find a property suited to your individual situation.

We mentioned before that there is a time to buy property and a time to sell it. Let's assume for a moment that you have learned the principles outlined in this book to the point where you have gone out and acquired a property. You are taking advantage of leverage, O.P.M., the income tax shelters available on your newly acquired property and any of the other benefits, such as equity buildup and cash return. Long-term ownership tends to diminish these advantages just as long-term ownership of an automobile tends to diminish the beneficial utility of the car.

In the case of income property, however, we're not talking about any diminishing physical aspects a property may have. Income properties can be properly maintained so that they are even more valuable in the future than when you originally purchased them. The diminishing values or benefits of property ownership are threefold.

They drop in the use of leverage because of loan reduction. This means you are using less "Other People's Money" and that you have more of your own money invested because you have been reducing the indebtedness. This means every dollar you have invested receives less return because the longer you hold the property, the greater your equity will probably be. Tax shelters usually decline the longer you hold the property. This is because most knowledgeable investors use methods of depreciating whereby depreciation is greater at the time the property is first purchased and then gradually decreases over the years of ownership. These two important factors are the reasons why the professional real estate investment counselor will tell you, "Don't

Marry Your Property." In order to recognize the proper time to sell, you should be in constant contact with your real estate investment counselor. He will keep abreast of the market for you, and at the same time he'll keep a running analysis of your property so that he will be able to advise you as to the proper course for disposition of your holdings. Generally speaking, the guidelines for knowing when to sell your property are these: 1. Whenever your net equity income rate drops 6 per cent from what it was originally; 2. When you have built up enough equity in the property to be able to afford approximately twice the size improved property than you now own; 3. Anytime you could obtain substantially more income tax advantages by selling or exchanging the property you now hold and acquiring a new one.

Take a look at the income property portrayed in the printout on page 124. Notice that in the initial year the property was purchased it was showing a tax loss of *$13,113* (Line 8, Col. 1), a net spendable income of *$39,853* (Line 13, Col. 1), a net equity income of *$46,929* (Line 18, Col. 1), with a net equity income rate of *13.04 per cent* (Line 20, Col. 1). Notice how these four factors decrease over the years of ownership. By the end of the fifth year, they have decreased to a positive taxable income of *$16,279* (Line 8, Col. 5), a net spendable income of *$37,165* (Line 13, Col. 5), equity income of *$46,473* (Line 18, Col. 5), and a net equity income rate of *10.11 per cent* (Line 20, Col. 5). Even though this property is a profitable investment for the owner, these figures dramatically illustrate what the years do to the financial advantages of ownership. It is also interesting to point out that up at the top of the computer printout, on line No. 1, Market Value, you will see that the property is actually growing in value. This, therefore, has increased the value of the asset, but, at the same time, diminished the leverage advantages to the owner. A good investment counselor could recommend to the owner if it was the best time to sell or exchange.

There are many factors that go into deciding when to advise a client that this time has come. However, knowledgeable real estate brokers and investment counselors are highly trained for this work. They can be of great value to an owner when advising him on this timing. Remember, to be successful in investments, you must not only be a good buyer, but just as important, a good seller.

Don't be afraid of the tax-free exchange provisions of the IRS code. Section 1031 of the tax code can have fabulous effect in helping you reach your goals. Let's see how an exchange might work.

PROPERTY ID: APARTMENT GARDENS

	1	2	3	4	5
***** BEGINNING OF YEAR—MARKET, LOAN & EQUITY STATUS *****					
1. MARKET VALUE	830000	846600	863532	880803	898419
LOAN #1	470000	462924	455347	447231	438540
LOAN #2	0	0	0	0	0
LOAN #3	0	0	0	0	0
2. TOTAL LOAN BALANCE	470000	462924	455347	447231	438540
3. EQUITY	360000	383676	408185	433572	459879
***** ANNUAL INCOME—EXPENSES—GROWTH *****					
4. CAPITALIZATION RATE (%)	9.05	9.04	9.04	9.04	9.04
5. NET OPERATING INCOME	75087	76533	78063	79625	81217
6. — INTEREST PAYMENTS	32092	31590	31053	30477	29860
7. — DEPRECIATION	56108	41849	38262	36629	35078
8. TAXABLE INCOME	-13113	3094	8749	12519	16279
9. NET OPERATING INCOME	75087	76533	78063	79625	81217
10. — P/I PAYMENTS	39168	39168	39168	39168	39168
11. GROSS SPENDABLE	35919	37365	38895	40457	42049
12. — INCOME TAX 30%	-3934	928	2625	3756	4884
13. NET SPENDABLE INCOME	39853	36436	36271	36701	37165
14. OPTIONAL CAP. IMPROVEMENT RES.	5000	5000	5000	5000	5000
15. NET SPENDABLE, LESS RESERVES	34853	31436	31271	31701	32165
16. NET SPENDABLE INCOME	39853	36436	36271	36701	37165
17. + PRINCIPAL PAYMENTS	7076	7578	8115	8691	9308
18. NET EQUITY INCOME	46929	44014	44386	45392	46473
19. NET EQ. INC. AS % OF ORIG. INVEST.	13.04	12.23	12.33	12.61	12.91
20. NET EQUITY INCOME RATE (%)	13.04	11.47	10.87	10.47	10.11
21. + EQUITY GROWTH RATE (%)	4.61	4.41	4.23	4.06	3.91
22. TOTAL EQUITY RATE (%)	17.65	15.88	15.11	14.53	14.01
***** CUM. PRINCIPAL—DEP.—SPENDABLE—EQUITY *****					
25. CUM. LOAN PAYMENTS TO PRINCIPAL	7076	14653	22769	31460	40768
26. CUM. TOTAL DEPRECIATION	56108	97957	136219	172848	207926
27. CUM. IMPROVEMENTS DEPREC.	36188	70967	103226	134253	163728
28. CUM. PERSONAL PROP. DEPREC.	19920	27390	32992	38595	44197
29. CUM. NET SPENDABLE	39853	76289	112560	149261	186426
30. CUM. NET EQUITY INCOME	46929	90943	135329	180721	227195
***** END OF YEAR TAX DETERMINATION ON SALE *****					
31. ADJUSTED COST BASIS	773892	732043	693781	657152	622074
32. CUM. DEP. — STRAIGHT LINE	30765	54891	79016	103141	127267
33. CUM. DEP. DIFF. (EXCESS)	65183	75436	83970	90872	96222
34. % EXCESS TAXED AS ORD INCOME	100.00	96.00	84.00	72.00	60.00
35. INDICATED GAIN — SALE/EXCHANGE	72708	131489	187021	241267	294313
36. TAXED AS ORD INC IF SOLD	56108	72418	70535	65428	57733
37. TAXED AS CAP GAIN AT SALE	16600	59070	116486	175839	236580
38. TAX ON ORD INCOME AT SALE	16832	21726	21161	19628	17320
39. TAX ON CAP GAIN AT SALE	2490	8861	17473	26376	35487
40. TOTAL TAX ON SALE	19322	30586	38633	46004	52807
41. EQUITY TO SELLERS IF SOLD	364353	377599	394938	413875	434349
42. EQUITY TO SELLERS IF EXCHANGED	383676	408185	433572	459879	487155
***** TAX DYNAMICS OF THE INVESTMENT *****					
43. TAXABLE GROSS SPENDABLE	0	3094	8749	12519	16279
44. TAXABLE PRINC. PYMNTS ON LOAN	0	0	0	0	0
45. PRE-TAX YIELD TO EQUAL LINE 13	56933	52052	51815	52430	53093
46. PRE-TAX RATE TO YIELD LINE 13	15.81	14.46	14.39	14.56	14.75
47. PRE-TAX YIELD TO EQUAL LINE 18	67041	62878	63409	64846	66390
48. PRE-TAX RATE TO YIELD LINE 18	18.62	17.47	17.61	18.01	18.44

Let's assume that originally you owned a twelve-unit apartment house, and you had held the property long enough so that you had almost doubled the original equity. It may be very possible for you to exchange it for a twenty-four-unit building in order to renew or increase your financial benefits from the ownership of this property. Your broker or real estate investment counselor will find a property suitable to this exchange. He will analyze the property, transferring your income tax applications into the new property. Again, with the use of a computer analysis, he will be able to show you how you will go on the three important types of income once you have made the exchange.

It is fair for you to ask at this time, "What if the owner of the twenty-four-unit doesn't want my twelve-unit?" It isn't necessary that he wants your twelve-unit. Your real estate broker or adviser can arrange for him to take the twelve-unit in exchange and line up a buyer for your twelve-unit so that the minute the owner of the twenty-four-unit apartment building receives your twelve-unit, he can turn right around on the same closing and deed it out to the purchaser. You have made a tax-free exchange, and the owner of the twenty-four-unit has merely made a cash-out sale, which, of course, will be taxable.

You might ask, "If taxes can be avoided, why would anyone want to sell out?" Again, this is a complicated point of income taxes, but your basis in the old property continues to go with you as you exchange. This means that you will be able to take less depreciation on the new property than you would if you had just purchased it outright for cash. As your exchanging pyramid goes along, there may come a time when your investment adviser says it is better for you to actually sell your existing holding and pay the tax on it. With the money left over, you might make another purchase. There are also lots of other motives involved besides money and income taxes that may require an outright cash sale.

People go into the market to sell properties outright for purposes of health, management, change in geographical location or the desire to raise immediate cash for other purposes. Therefore, it is possible to find income property owners willing to accept a cash-out regardless of the income tax implications. The best advice that you can get in this area, of course, will come from a real estate investment counselor or a well-trained, knowledgeable real estate broker.

Anybody who wants to have his money working for him, who understands that he must invest, would do well to investigate the ramifications of improved income property ownership. There is an income property for every purpose. There is an income property for nearly every degree of risk and nearly every type of yield. Some will take management on your part. Others will not. Some are high risk properties, others have practically no risk to safety of capital. Some have very high yields and are inflation-proof, whereas other types of property will yield income that is subject to erosion via inflation and has moderate or low yields. But, generally speaking, income property will have greater growth and yield possibilities than nearly any other kind of investment.

There is a point of pride in the ownership of income property. It's nice to drive by it and know that those tenants are actually in there worrying about how to pay you the rent so that you might make all your expenses, reduce your indebtedness, and build your estate. It's nice to be able to show your friends this property and say, "Even while I was asleep last night, that building over there was making me money and helping build my estate."

The future of income property looks even greater than it has in the past. The United States government has made a survey which said that before the year 2000 every building that has ever existed in the U.S. and that exists today will have to be duplicated to meet the need for the shelter of commerce, people, industry and business. Just think of it. Every skyscraper, warehouse, factory, log cabin, A-frame home and shopping center will have to be duplicated between now and the year 2000. Never before has there been such a sparkling opportunity for investors to enjoy high yields, tax benefits, low risk and O.P.M. as there exists in our time.

Right now, throughout the United States, apartment buildings, office and shopping center complexes, as well as other income properties, are coming under tremendous buying pressures. This influx of money is coming from the Middle East, Holland, Canada, Germany, and even England. These foreign investors are well aware of what we have been telling you in this book: that existing properties are good buys. But this buying pressure is driving up the prices of income properties to the point where there is no longer any cash flow. In fact, most buildings sold today have a cash deficit. These investors expect to be able to raise the rent in three to five years and make up for these conditions at that time. So, if you are going to invest in income properties today—be ready for this severe competition in buying—it is a seller's market. Not even a recession is likely to affect this market because no one can build cheaper—development is tough, utilities are scarce. Move with caution, get knowledgeable advice.

Even the doom-peddling life insurance companies understand the great potential, the great future, and the low risk involved in the ownership of income-producing property. That's why they are willing to make 70–80 per cent loans on these properties. They know that they increase in value, have an extremely low foreclosure rate, and are highly profitable in the right hands. Make your move now. You don't have to know how to analyze a property to its last detail. You don't have to know all the income tax ramifications. You don't have to know how to create a property analysis and a projection on income property or even interpret a computer printout. Find a local C.C.I.M. or a knowledgeable real estate broker. Ask him if he understands these processes. If he does, let him be your technician and do your work for you. In 99.9 cases of property transfer it's the seller who pays the commission, and you can have all of this investment advice, years of experience, at no cost to you. What an opportunity! What an ideal situation. Begin your course toward spending your later years in that magic triangle known as the "Other 5 per cent."

Take the first step now. Get a true professional on your team. Most real estate brokers are house salesmen. You need something more. Find one that is experienced and knowledgeable in the field of investments. The following will help you find the proper adviser. These are institutions that award designations to people within the real estate business who are skilled in its many aspects. Seek out the one that fits your needs.

CCIM. (Certified Commercial Investment Member)—one who has studied investment and commercial real estate.

SIR. (Society of Industrial Realtors)—experts in the analysis and marketing of industrial properties.

MAI. (Members Appraisal Institute)—experts in the evaluation of all types of real estate.

CRB. (Certified Residential Broker)—experts in marketing homes.

AFLB. (Accredited Farm and Land Brokers)—experts and specialists in marketing and analysis of farm, ranch and raw land properties.

CPM. (Certified Property Managers)—the professionals of property management.

SRA. (Society of Residential Appraisers)—experts in the evaluation of mostly residential properties.

(These designations are only given to people who have passed extensive training and who belong to the above professional organizations.)

CHAPTER 11

MANAGEMENT

If you have done any investigation into real estate for an investment you have undoubtedly read that one of the greatest problems with the ownership of income property is management. Any good stockbroker will tell you that before he makes a final decision as to what stock position to acquire for his portfolio, he will make an in-depth study of management. As a matter of fact, the entire idea of investing is to bring money under good management. When you select a mutual fund you are in fact saying, "People managing that fund can do a better job with my money than I can." This also holds true when you select an individual stock. You are saying, "The management of the company in which I am buying stock is more capable of making my money grow than I am." In good times and bad there is always capital money to invest in those enterprises that have demonstrated they have topnotch and high-quality management to make money grow.

Over the years most investment advisers and counselors have advised against the purchase of real estate because it presents such a big management problem. If you are successful at your chosen career you probably find that there is not enough time for you to do all the things that you hope to do. Possibly you would like to give your business even more time than you are already giving it. Of course, you need time for your family, and there is always your favorite recreational activity that requires time, too. How in the world can you go into an income property investment that requires heavy management? No wage earner, professional or busy investor wants to saddle himself with even more demand on his time; and some say that is what income property takes. Of course, there are those people whose time will allow them to look after income property. However, they are generally not the people who have large sums of money to invest in real estate, unless they are retired and are looking for something to do. When these investment counselors and money advisers state that real estate is not for the average investor because of its management responsibilities, they are overlooking some new and remarkable innovations to a blossoming business within the real estate industry called professional management.

Very few investment advisers who are actually knowledgeable in all fields of investment can deny that real estate is probably the very best investment available on the market today. If they were honest in their advice they would have to point out that there are two primary weaknesses to real estate:

1. It requires direct and responsive management.
2. There is a fantastic lack of professional knowledge within the real estate industry itself to provide the investor with sound guidance.

Let's consider the fact of real estate management.

Basically, there are two kinds of management in real estate. There is the do-it-yourself kind and there is professional management. Before you pooh-pooh the do-it-yourself type management, you should consider these important factors. There are good low-risk, high-yield income properties that are too small to afford professional management. There are many people who have the time and talent to manage real estate, although they are not professionals within the industry. There are properties in which it is absolutely an economic necessity for the owner to do his own management. This is particularly true when the owner has bought a piece of property on such high leverage (O.P.M.) that he needs every dime out of the property to meet necessary overhead and debt service or mortgage payments. There is the possibility of obtaining an on-site or resident caretaker who can do all of the heavy management for an owner, leaving the owner with only the responsibility of managing the caretaker. This can greatly reduce the time an owner has to spend in the operation of his property. The subject of caretakers is in itself a very interesting study. Just as all employees, or personnel in any business operation, require management, so do resident managers or caretakers.

It is important that these caretakers have a basic knowledge of people, have a basic knowledge of maintenance, and have enough sales ability to keep the property suitably occupied. Of course there are many other facets to good property management. However, the items listed above are reasons for do-it-yourself management. As previously stated, probably the worst thing that can happen to you from the financial standpoint is to not own any property that produces income. If it comes down to a choice between not owning any property and/or having to manage it yourself, there should be no doubt in your mind that you should make time in your schedule to buy income properties and manage your own. To merely say that instead of buying income property you are going to buy raw land in order to avoid all management is to kid yourself. Granted, raw land takes less management, but it does take some. In order for anyone to understand the full ramifications of income property it is first necessary to know what good management is.

WHAT *IS* GOOD MANAGEMENT?

Basically, the management of any successful enterprise boils down to two items: the maximizing of income, and the minimizing of expenses. These two items could sum up good management in a nutshell. However, many volumes of books and courses have been given to educate people to the point of being capable of accomplishing these two important elements of management. Let's take an example as it applies to income property.

In order to maximize profits you must know your competition; you must know the fair market value of the rentals you are offering to the public; you must do continual market research to make sure your rental pricing is in line; you must constantly survey the physical attributes of your property; you must properly maintain them for the amount of rental you are charging; and, on top of that, you must know how and when and what kind of improvements to make and how much money to spend on maintenance, or you'll over-improve and find yourself in a position of not being able to reap a fair return on your investment. Furthermore, to maximize income you should know about financing, property taxes, credit, civil rights laws, rental collections, lease or rental agreements, food accounting methods and tax laws.

On the other hand, if you are to perform the second important element of management, the minimizing of expenses, you are going to have to know another great multitude of items which will help you accomplish this goal. Some of these items are taxation, the purchasing of materials and labor, human psychology, personnel management, the ins and outs of real estate financing, the physical and mechanical maintenance of property, contracting, advertising, promotion, public relations and personnel training. All of these items go into good management. They apply to most businesses, regardless of who is acting as the owner or executive. Surprisingly enough, one of the best ways to learn all about management is by actually practicing the art.

Of course, it can be a very expensive lesson. This long list of items necessary for good management is not meant to scare you away from purchasing real estate and managing it yourself. It is only meant to point out what you can be faced with in property management so you can weigh these items against all the reasons we give you for a do-it-yourself project. Naturally, the degree of exercise and understanding of these elements will be in direct proportion to the size and type of the property you select for your portfolio.

For example, a warehouse leased to a responsible tenant on a net, net basis (tenant takes care of everything) will require practically no management on the part of the owner. On the other hand, a two-, three-, or four-unit apartment building could require the owner to practice a great deal of the elements set forth under good management. As we have stated, even raw land needs management, not from the standpoint that you have to hire a caretaker and supervise him or collect rent and supervise tenants, but from the standpoint that you must be in constant contact with the circumstances and occurrences going on in the neighborhood in which the property is located. You are going to have to watch any change in traffic patterns or zoning or other improvements that are going on in the neighborhood that might affect your property. You might also have to be concerned with possible land improvements such as sewer, water, curbs, streets, gas, electricity, payments, restrictions, and other elements that might affect the value or serviceability of your raw land holdings. As an alternate to all these things on a do-it-yourself basis is this booming new business within the real estate industry called Professional Management. Let's investigate this service and see how it might help you accomplish your investment goals.

PROFESSIONAL MANAGEMENT

Professional management is a service performed by someone who is a professional in the real estate business and who is willing to perform duties for the owners of properties for a predetermined fee or percentage of the gross income. This service is generally offered by real estate brokers and/or separate professional management companies equipped to perform all of the duties an owner would have to assume if it were not for the professional management agency.

Just as in the case of any other service or commodity, there are both good professional managers and incompetent ones. Owners have to be extremely careful with the selection of the property managers they hire. Within nearly every city there are firms that are ready, willing and able to perform the duties of professional managers. It has only been in recent years that most real estate brokers engaged in the commercial, industrial and investment areas of real estate have taken the duties of professional management seriously. Recent years have seen an upgrading in the educational facilities available to the professional managers. One organization in particular has done a great deal to advance the quality of professional management in the United States.

This organization is the Institute for Real Estate Management which is affiliated with the Realtors National Marketing Institute. They instituted a program to educate their members. Those who qualified earned the professional status of CPM (Certified Property Managers). The courses and requirements to obtain this professional management are being upgraded constantly. In general, the CPM's are doing an outstanding job of raising the level of the services available within the industry.

What services are normally performed by the professional property manager? In short, managers are ordered to take over all the duties normally attributed to the owner, but with the full-time professional touch. Generally speaking, they are better equipped to do the job than an owner because they *are* in the business full time. Management institutions should be able to tell at what price level each rental property should be maintained, and be able to meet and anticipate competition that might be occurring in the general area. They normally provide professional accounting records to the owners, keeping an accurate statement of all income and expenses. They hire, train and act as counsel to on-property resident managers. They do everything possible to maximize income and minimize expenses.

Yet, at the same time, they maintain and preserve the capital asset and its value. One of the ways in which they can minimize expenses is through mass buying of materials and labor. If they are honest, they pass the savings on to the owner. Also, they can serve the owner in an advisory capacity on refinancing, taxation, selling, exchanging, remodeling, upgrading, decorating, advertising, and public relations. If the property is larger, and falls into the classifications that generally call for professional management, it can be said in general that the professional manager should be able to more than pay for his own services and make the investment property ownership worry-free to the owners. It stands to reason that if the professional manager can buy labor, equipment and materials, advertising and accounting services cheaper because he is doing it in mass volume, it is not too difficult to understand how the professional manager can more than pay for any expenses he adds to the ownership of the property.

One of the big reasons why most real estate brokers, even though they are engaged in the investment, commercial and industrial field, have not provided property management in the past is this: It is largely an unprofitable service. However, most brokers hope to obtain benefits for their services, but not through the direct management of income properties. They stand a good chance of eventually obtaining a listing on the property, and they hope to make a profit on commissions for handling sales or exchanges. In recent time, however, brokers are finding that management can be profitable if it is highly professionalized. One of the most recent innovations in income property management that has helped make it profitable to the broker, and at the same time more advantageous to the owner, is the use of computers in accounting. It used to take a whole factory of bookkeepers to do the tremendous task of collecting all the funds and paying all the expenses but now it is possible to use computers to perform the services formerly done by a large clerical staff. Even though there has been a general upgrading of services and educational levels of professional property managers, there are still many services and much education needed in this field. The owner would do himself a great favor by closely checking out the available professional managers before he makes the final selection of the one who is going to manage his property.

Here are some of the questions you can ask yourself before signing a contract with a professional management firm: What system do they have for training and hiring caretakers? Do they have a job description for the caretaker to follow so that he knows exactly what his duties will be? Do they have a formal training program for caretakers and a written manual to guide and educate caretakers in the performance of their duties? After all, it is impossible for anyone to do a good job in anything if they do not know what is expected of them.

Take a good look at their method of reporting the accounting of the property. How often is the accounting given? Does the management report to the owner give him a full account of what is happening on the property? This report should not only include the source of all income and the itemized expenditure of all expenses, but a status of the loan and a written narrative on what has happened to the property as far as the management was concerned during the reporting period.

Many good property management firms will give a narrative report to the owner telling him how his property was managed during the most recent accounting period. This means an explanation of any significant occurrence and, if necessary, a request for advice or permission to make any significant changes based on the advice of the professional property manager that are not normally covered in the professional management contract between the owner and the manager.

Does the professional manager bond all the employees responsible for handling money whether it's within or without their own firm? This should include the caretaker of the property. Does the professional management firm have a good system for keeping an accurate inventory of any personal or equipment items necessary to the income or maintenance of the building? How often does the professional manager make periodic inspections of the property, and what method does he use for keeping track of these inspections? What consulting services does his firm offer in the way of marketing analysis, advertising, public relations, refinancing, selling, exchanging and taxation?

Probably the most important of all, does he have a system by which he runs the income and expenses of the property according to a preconceived budget? Just as it is with anything else in life, it is very difficult to reach a predetermined target unless you know what that goal or target is. Today's good professional managers predetermine a budget and set forth how they think the property will produce as to income versus expenses. In many cases this is now being done by computer. Budget reports are being mailed along with regular management reports at periodic, predetermined times so that the owner can tell whether the property is running close to the income and expenses as it was set forth when the owner undertook the professional manager; and the owner will be able to tell whether there was too little or too much maintenance on the building and whether the vacancies are running higher than originally intended. If so, what can be done to correct this situation? Furthermore, the budgets will tell how much under or over every single itemized expense is, so that the proper action may be taken to correct an unfavorable situation. Of course, the budget will probably have to be changed every year in accordance with marketing conditions.

Any firm that does not perform this budget service is not doing all it could to make its services an asset rather than an expense. There is one other advantage to the budget. It provides a track record which helps tell when the property should be sold, exchanged, upgraded or remodeled, and it provides all the background necessary to effect a verbal sale when it becomes necessary to do so. If you can say that the firm you have hired to perform professional management services on your income property has done this, then you probably have a service that will undoubtedly provide a higher-quality service than you could supply . . . even if you knew the field and had the time to do it. Of course, the final and most important factor in selecting a professional property manager is to inspect the buildings he already manages. Go see these properties and find out if they are clean, occupied, well maintained, etc. The proof is in the seeing!

THE ADVANTAGES OF PROFESSIONAL PROPERTY MANAGERS

As previously stated, the professional manager can more than pay his own way when he is properly performing his function. With good professional management the ownership of any type of real estate can become completely passive. In other words, it should not require any particular time or talent from the owner in order to have a successful investment.

If the investment counselors or advisers who warned the public against buying income property knew how the new and modern professional property manager can help an owner, they would be forced into admitting that there are very few investments which can even come close to real estate.

There are thousands of investors across the United States who have never even been inside the properties they own. Some of them don't even live within thousands of miles of the property, yet they have the assurance that their property is being well managed because they took the time to select a good professional property manager. It is possible that you could take on the investment in any income property by placing it in the hands of the truly professional real estate manager and have, in every respect, a passive investment just like those offered to you in the ownership of corporate bonds, mutual funds, stock, or even savings accounts. The management or supervision of income properties has become one of the most critical elements in the failure or success of real property. Owners, professional and amateurs alike, have strived over the years to reach a scientific approach to the accomplishment of the two primary functions of property management—maximizing profits and minimizing expenses. Overemphasis of either function can cause poor performance of the property just as underemphasis can cause dissatisfied ownership.

In recent years it has become more and more evident that the field of property management belongs either in the hands of well-trained people or in the hands of the true professional. Professional management concerns itself with all the elements that make any business successful. Business success must be predicated on one important factor: A customer must receive adequate rewards for the product or service it renders.

Historically, the property manager did only what was absolutely necessary to fill vacancies and spent as little money as possible to keep the tenant. This attitude resulted in a constant battle between owner and renter. The heat and light was provided in as minimum quantities as possible. Repairs were made only when absolutely essential. Competition alone dictated to the owner the amount of services he had to provide to keep his building occupied. Now the entire concept has changed. The professional manager knows that he is dealing in the total concept of living, not just providing shelter—especially in the case of apartment building management.

It is the job of the professional to create an atmosphere conducive to good living on an economic scale justified by the rental rates. This total living concept encompasses many tasks, and it requires the professional to use every modern method of management available. A list of these methods and tools graphically illustrates just what vast experience, training and knowledge must be employed:

1, Human relations
2. Economics
3. Accounting
4. Advertising and promotion
5. Systems and records
6. Salesmanship
7. Marketing, research and forecasting
8. Art, decorating, aesthetics
9. Construction
10. Education
11. Buying
12. Principles of human management

These broad fields must be mastered by the professional property manager. It must be done on a basis that accomplishes the two basic and primary functions of management. Good property managers understand and appreciate all these important factors. There are new and dynamic firms and personnel entering this field. With a little investigation nearly every community can offer the real estate investor good professional property management.

So, from now on, if you hear from any professional or semi-professional investment counselor or adviser that you should stay away from the ownership of improved income-producing real estate, don't you believe it. Modern techniques and dedication to doing a good job are rapidly making real estate a non-time-consuming passive investment. That spells profits and opportunities for the income property owner.

CHAPTER 12

GROUP INVESTING

Group investing has come, gone, and returned. It's accomplishing in real estate what the mutual fund did in the stock market. It's obtaining higher yields yet lower risks. It's obtaining more predictability and making investments with larger growth available to investors regardless of their available investment capital.

There was a time when the average investor absolutely shuddered when he heard the word *partnership*. However, the new concept in real estate has chased away the bogeyman and dispelled old fears.

WHAT IS GROUP INVESTING?

We prefer to call real estate syndications "group investing" because it more graphically illustrates just what is available in the field of real estate investments. How would you like to walk into a stockbroker's office and tell him that you would buy a certain stock if he also bought some of the same stock with you? Furthermore, let's say you bought the stock on margin. You make an agreement with the stockbroker that if there is ever a margin call, he would loan you all the money required in the call. But that is not all. You further get him to agree that if the stock is sold for less money than it cost, he would first have to give you back as much of your money from the sale as possible before he could take out a dime. Just try it. Just walk into your favorite stockbroker's office and tell him you are willing to invest on this type of situation.

After the men in white jackets arrive to take you away, you will know that the only place this kind of investment is available is in the field of real estate.

Modern real estate brokers throughout the United States are making available to their clients this dynamic method of investing. First of all, let's understand the rationale of group investing. The United States itself could not have achieved leadership in the world if it were not for the countless number of people that join together to achieve common goals. Insurance companies, large corporations, banks, and most utilities have one thing in common. They represent the combined investments of the many different people who have contributed capital to make these enterprises possible. Group investing is not really new.

For those who wish to invest in real estate, the principle of group investing is also applicable. Several people pooling capital can move into more profitable areas of real estate investing. Few persons can do it alone, but several can do it together. Several investments may be formed from either land or income purchases. It is part of our American heritage to think big. It is an attitude of accomplishment that separates the wealthy from those just getting by.

Group investment is the best way of making a real estate broker or real estate investment counselor put his money where his mouth is. It's a way of telling him that, yes, you are willing to invest with him providing that he is so sure of his purchase that he is willing to take the larger share of risk.

WHAT ARE THE ADVANTAGES OF GROUP INVESTING?

First of all, once you know the most common type of real estate syndicate you will see that participating in group investment lets you receive a great deal of diversification of your capital. This reduces risk. Next, it's a well-known fact that larger properties usually yield larger profits. It's pretty tough in today's high income tax, fast-living society to accumulate large sums of cash. Oh, don't feel badly, it happens to the wage earner, and it happens to the big corporation executive making thousands upon thousands of dollars a year.

Modes of living, new inventions and luxuries, and an ever-increasingly affluent society seem to rake off most of that extra cash you would like to be saving for investment purposes. Group investing is one way that you can use a small amount of capital, sit back with no management responsibilities, and see your investment capital grow. One of the other big advantages to group investing is that you can buy larger properties, and larger properties afford full-time professional management, as we discussed in the last chapter.

This in itself is a sufficient advantage to command your attention. There's one other advantage. The group investment usually has a greater degree of liquidity than does individual ownership. This is accomplished because there is usually one or more of your partners willing to buy your share, and your investment counselor or broker doesn't have to go out into the general market to find a buyer for your interest. He simply offers it to the other partners and completes the transfer for your interest. Many real estate investors are discovering that they can find good positions in the investment property for as little as $500. Now we admit that the average is usually $5,000 or more, but there are companies and groups being formed that can take in the young struggling junior executive or the capital-short widow on as little as $2,000 to $10,000.

THE METHODS OF GROUP INVESTING

There are several forms of group investments. They are generally classified in these three ways:

1. Corporation
2. Joint venture
3. Limited partnership

Each of these legal vehicles has advantages and disadvantages. Let's investigate them.

THE CORPORATION

The corporation is a separate legal entity granted life usually by a state government. According to the law, it is a complete and separate person, and it is to be treated as such. Its advantages are—first—ownership in the entity, represented by stock certificates. This means that it is generally easy to acquire ownership in a corporation and those interests are usually highly transferable, which makes for generally good liquidity. Another advantage to the corporation is that it has perpetual life. It doesn't die like a real person, but it can go out of existence through dissolution or bankruptcy.

The corporation also offers central management which usually means that there is a Board of Directors and an officer responsible for seeing that the corporation accomplishes its purposes. Limitation of liability is another one of the corporation's advantages. In other words, corporations usually sell non-assessable stock, which means that the investors cannot be required to add any additional funds in case the corporation suffers adverse financial conditions.

The corporation does have some disadvantages. It is taxed by the Internal Revenue Service as a separate entity. This means that the corporation must pay taxes on what it earns, and it cannot pass on any tax loss to the individual investor.

There are many forms of corporations. There is one kind of corporation, particularly popular in the real estate investment field, that is known as a Real Estate Investment Trust. This is a special creature created by an Act of Congress. The law simply states that this corporation can pass on tax losses (shelters) to the owner. To qualify as a real estate investment trust, the corporation must have 100 or more owners and stockholders, and it must distribute 90 per cent of its net earnings. This can be a disadvantage to the owner because it does not allow the investment trust to accumulate large sums of capital to increase its ownership position.

Anyone truly interested in the real estate investment corporation can find adequate information at his local stock brokerage company. There are many real estate investment trusts listed on various exchanges throughout the country. One needs only to go down to the stockbroker and ask him for a prospectus on these various real estate and investment trusts offering stock to the public.

To those of you who are looking for rapid growth and tax shelter, the real estate investment trust still is not the answer. It is tightly regulated as to the amount of depreciation and the type of investment it can make. So often, a real estate investment trust starts out by making purchases of equities in real estate and ends up being nothing more than a mortgage lender, subjecting its investors to a fixed rate type of investment. We know what that means, having learned what inflation can do to fixed rate investments. Of course, there are times when the real estate investor interested in growth will want to participate in a corporation. This is particularly true in the case of development where doing it on an individual basis would cause the owner to be declared by the

Internal Revenue Service as a dealer. A dealer in real estate is one who is not an investor. He cannot take the advantageous capital gains position when it comes to paying his income taxes. The Internal Revenue Service says that dealers are merely holding property such as any other merchant would inventory. Therefore, all profits are subject to ordinary income taxes. Even with these disadvantages, it is easy to see that if you were going into a development type of project that might subject you to becoming a dealer it would be wise to use the corporation method for real estate investing. However, to the large majority of the public, neither the real estate investment trust nor any corporation is an adequate vehicle for group investment. There are other methods better suited to accomplishing the specific investment goals of growth, tax shelter, limitation of liability, risk and yield.

JOINT VENTURE

A joint venture is a partnership created for a specific purpose. It, too, has many advantages and disadvantages. Some of the tax advantages can pass on directly to the individual partners. It is a vehicle allowing several people to join together and share in all risks and profits while pooling their money to accomplish one central task. There are some very heavy limitations, however, on the joint venture.

Generally speaking, it has no central management. This means that when an important decision must be arrived at to make the property a success, all the partners must agree according to their original joint venture agreement. This can delay a decision which could be costly in real estate. Joint venture does not have perpetual life. It ends at the death of any one partner. Joint venture interests are extremely difficult to transfer because the partners are usually limited very severely in the transferability of interests. Just as in the case of the corporation, however, there are specific reasons why you might want to have a joint venture. The main feature of this legal vehicle is the willingness of all partners to assume equal risks, management and liability.

THE LIMITED PARTNERSHIP

Of all legal vehicles used in forming real estate group investments, probably the limited partnership offers more advantages to the real estate investor than any other. Generally speaking, the limited partnership does allow many of the advantages not available in any of the other legal organizations we have mentioned thus far. Historically speaking, the limited partnership grew up from English law. It simply meant this—one or more of the partners were going to be completely responsible for all the work in management it took to make the partnership a success, and they were called general partners. The limited partners were not to take any voice in management, but they were to invest their money. It does mean that the limited partner could never be asked to contribute any more capital than originally agreed.

The limited partnership offers all the partners the advantages of being able to take tax shelters directly. In other words, all tax advantages pass directly through the individual partners, although the transferability of interests is not quite so easy as it is in a corporation. Generally speaking, the limited partnership does allow a reasonable latitude in the transferability of the individual partner's interest. As far as management is concerned, the general partner (or partners) is the sole management. As a matter of fact, the limited partners can destroy their limitation of liability by taking part in any active management decision.

The continuity of the limited partnership is generally for a predesignated length of time and only ceases to exist at the end of that time or upon dissolution or upon the death, bankruptcy or the declaration of insanity of the general partner. Many of the gleaming stone and glass skyscrapers you see in Manhattan are owned by limited partnerships. It has become extremely popular over the last few decades to use limited partnerships in the acquisition of property. For the average real estate investor very few legal vehicles will present themselves that are equal to or better than the investment in the limited partnership.

The limited partnership agreement can, of course, be written in countless ways. Some of the more popular methods today include such amiable advantages to the limited partner as these: The general partner is usually the professional real estate counselor or broker. He goes out into the market and selects a piece of property. After proper investigation, he selects it as the ideal investment for the partnership. The general partner may use his own funds to option or some other way obtain the right to purchase this property. In the course of the formation of the limited partnership, it is set forth that he is to be the sole manager of the property, and is responsible for any losses over and above the original contributions of capital. By responsibility we mean that the general partner can be required to either give or loan the partnership enough money to operate in the event of operating loss. Other than what is agreed upon by the limited partners as to their original contribution, the general partner can in no way go back and ask the limited partner to share in any losses the partnership might incur. The general partner invests his own money, assumes responsibility for the management and operation of the property, takes the majority of physical responsibility, and manages the partnership.

In the case of really confident general partners, they subordinate their interests to the limited partners. This, in essence, means that if the property is ever liquidated, all the limited partners get their original contribution back before the general partner receives any of his capital. This does not mean that he does not participate equally in any income the property might produce. The general partner usually charges the partnership a regular professional management fee for the management of the property during the time it is held by the partnership. If the general partner is actually confident in the property he is buying, he will not mind investing his money and assuming the extra liabilities and responsibilities. That leaves the limited partner in this position: He invests the money for his initial capital, but he does not have to assume any further responsibility or liability.

FORMING THE GROUP

An investment group may be formed to buy a specific property recommended by the professional real estate investment counselor or broker, or the group may be formed first so that the professional can then go out and find the properties that best suit the goal of the partnership. There has been a great deal of talk about the disadvantages of any kind of partnership. The big disadvantage is that partners often disagree as to the overall objective or goal of the partnership. This can be avoided by the professional syndicator or real estate broker who provides each of the potential partners with a thorough and professional counseling service before they are commited to any type of investment in a limited partnership.

For example, limited partnerships may be formed for growth and tax shelter or they may be formed simply for cash income or any combination of these. It stands to reason that the investment counselor who is knowledgeable in his field would not put a widow requiring cash income into a highly leveraged property that was good only for tax shelter in long-term growth. Here is one area that is so often neglected by the syndicator. *Counseling is essential* in order to form a compatible investment group. Only after counseling can a specific group be recommended to an individual. Do not attempt to buy any part of any investment group unless your real estate investment counselor has properly determined your goals and can show you property analyses and projections that the property is likely to help you reach those investment goals.

SOME POINTS TO REMEMBER ABOUT THE LIMITED PARTNERSHIP

If the investment real estate counselor or real estate broker has true confidence in the property he is presenting to you, he won't mind taking on the extra responsibility and liability it takes to be the general partner. After all, there are several advantages to him in forming the group. If this wasn't so, he could not afford to participate in any of these group investments. The general partner will go into the market and obtain a suitable property. This can be done before or after the partnership has been formed.

In most cases he will use his own money to obtain an option on the property, or in some other way obtain first rights to buy it. If he is ethical he will have to tell the seller that he is purchasing the property for a group that he represents, and from that standpoint may or may not accept a commission from the seller. In the event he is buying the property net as to commissions he will mark the property up, generally speaking, from 8 per cent to 12 per cent on improved property, and 10 per cent to 25 per cent on unimproved properties. This markup represents fees for his effort and risk while acquiring the property and forming the group. His only other compensation will be in managing the property. The fee usually is 5 per cent to 7 per cent of the gross income the property produces, or from $1,000 to $5,000 a year for managing unimproved property. These are small considerations in comparison to benefits the limited partner can receive by joining investment groups. You have put the professional on the hook, limited your liabilities, increased your chances for liquidity, obtained professional management to the highest degree, and, at the same time, received professional counseling which should help direct you to your overall financial goal.

OTHER FUNCTIONS OF THE GENERAL PARTNER

As the professional manager for the property and the partnership, the general partner will see to it that you get predetermined periodic statements as to the condition of the partnership and the property. He will also be responsible for hiring an accountant to audit the books at the end of the year, and he'll send you partnership income tax returns as prepared by the accountant. The accountant's fee is generally paid from the partnership funds. However, the general partner is responsible for seeing that the accountant gets all the information necessary for him to construct the income tax return. Once these income tax returns are received, you simply incorporate them in the other portions of your income tax return. This makes group investing strictly a passive type of investment with all the advantages available only in real estate.

HOW THE PROFESSIONAL SYNDICATOR PRESENTS INVESTMENT POSSIBILITY TO POTENTIAL INVESTORS

The truly professional real estate investment broker or real estate investment counselor will show the prospective investor a complete brochure describing the income expenses and important physical attributes of the property. He will also present a ten-year projection, as shown in the section on Income Property, a recap of the advantages of ownership, and a copy of the partnership papers prepared by competent legal advisers. In the vast majority of cases the limited partner will probably not even deem it necessary to make a physical inspection of the property.

It also makes no difference where the property is located geographically in group investing. The investor can purchase property in any part of the United States, as long as he knows that he has a responsible and professional general partner to manage the property. This in itself is a great advantage as far as diversification is concerned.

OTHER PROTECTIONS FOR THE LIMITED PARTNER

Generally speaking, most limited partnership agreements will provide that the general partner can be removed upon a 60 per cent to 85 per cent vote of the limited partners. This means that if for any reason the general partner (or partners) is not performing satisfactorily, the limited partners can join together in removing him from his office. Of course, they cannot take away his portion of the investment in the property, but they can form a new group with a different general partner that better suits their management requirements. Furthermore, some states allow corporations to be the general partners. In this case, the limited partners have the added advantage of having the general partner a corporation, which usually has more than one person in charge and perpetual

life. This varies from state to state, and it is unfortunate that it's
not available to group investors in every state.

In summary, here are the tremendous advantages in participating in a limited partnership.

1. You have a professional investing with you and taking the majority of the risks and responsibilities.
2. You can receive diversification.
3. You can have all the tax advantages that would be
   available if you were the single owner.
4. You can participate in profits from larger properties
   through the benefits of pooling money.
5. General partnerships generally have greater liquidity
   than even individual real estate ownership.
6. You can use the same wonderful investment
   techniques available to individual owners, such as
   leverage.
7. You can obtain a higher degree of predictability because you can be assured that if the general partner is
   going to assume a greater responsibility and liability,
   he will be willing to do a much more thorough
   analysis of the property before purchasing it.
8. In many cases, you can receive subordination from
   the general partner, which means you get your money
   back before he gets any of his back in case of liquidation.

The advantages of the limited partnership and group investing
in real estate are not available in many other fields. It is the
salvation of the small investor, as far as real estate is concerned,
and it's a sparkling opportunity for the large investor to limit his
risks, obtain professional management and diversify his capital.

You don't have to know much about real estate, tax laws,
management or any of the other technicalities that go into making
a decision on the purchase of investment property. *All you have
to know is the reputation and reliability of the general partner.*
You can do this by investigating him through banks, credit
agencies and other investors; by studying his past record; and, of
course, looking at his professional qualifications. At this very
moment there are thousands of people from every walk of life
enjoying the benefits of group property investment—airplane
pilots, doctors, clergy, drill press operators, welders, school
teachers, dentists and dogcatchers. All take advantage of this
marvelous, painless way to own improved or unimproved real

	INDIVIDUAL 4 Unit	GROUP INVESTMENT Per Partner (4%)	32 Unit Total
Price	$34,500	$28,000	$700,000
First Loan	24,500	18,000	450,000
Equity	$10,000	$10,000	$250,000
PROPERTY INCOME ANALYSIS			
Gross Scheduled Income	$ 4,720	$ 4,563	$114,062
Less: Vacancy Allowance	480	225	5,631
Gross Operating Income	4,240	4,338	108,431
Less: Operating Costs	1,993	1,596	39,900
NET Operating Income	$ 2,247	$ 2,742	$ 68,531
OWNERSHIP ANALYSIS OF BOTH PROPERTIES			
Taxable Income			
Net Operating Income	$ 2,247	$ 2,742	$ 68,531
Less: Interest Payments	1,653	2,051	26,280
Less: Depreciation	1,560	1,900	47,512
NET Taxable			
Income (Loss)	$ (966)	$ (209)	$ (5,261)
SPENDABLE INCOME (Cash)			
NET Operating Income	$ 2,247	$ 2,742	$ 68,531
Less: Principal and			
Interest Payments	2,400	1,642	41,050
Gross Spendable Income	(153)	$ 1,100	$ 27,481
Less: Income Tax			
30% Bracket	(290)	(63)	(1,578)
NET Spendable			
NET Spendable Annually	$ 137	$ 1,163	$ 29,059
EQUITY-INCOME			
Net Operating Income	$ 2,247	$ 2,742	$ 68,531
Less: Interest on Loan	1,653	1,051	26,280
Less: Income Tax			
(Saving)	(290)	(63)	(1,578)
NET Equity Income	$ 884	$ 1,754	$ 43,829
Return on $10,000			
Investment	8.84%	17.5%	17.5%

The above figures show you that ownership of one interest in a syndication will give you the **same percentage return as ownership of the entire property.** They also reveal that, in this instance, **the return on the $10,000 investment is almost twice as much in the syndicate** as the return on the four-unit. Combine the income advantages with that of being management free and you can readily see some of the advantages syndication offers the small investor.

This illustration compares what a person with $10,000 can do individually or by participating in a syndication. The choice between the two is available to the person with $10,000.

estate. Investigate it now. Once you have found the proper professional counselor or knowledgeable real estate broker you have an acre of diamonds in your own back yard. And you'll get rich while sleeping!

To see the advantages offered by group investing, take a look at the following example presented by Joe Harrington, a Denver real estate investment counselor. The figures in the preceeding chart compare what an individual who has $10,000 can do by investing through group investment (syndication) as opposed to buying a four-unit apartment by himself.

STOCKBROKER'S OFFERINGS

Many big and financially stable security houses are offering interests in limited partnerships they have put together and are underwriting. Many of these partnerships are doing well; others have failed. These failures are mostly a result of the lack of experience in real estate on the part of the stockbrokers and the general partners that are in charge. Proceed with caution, but bear in mind that you will probably be better off investing with one local, knowledgeable and trustworthy real estate broker.

CHAPTER 13

OTHER PEOPLE'S MONEY

With all the advantages of real estate ownership, the three factors that stand out head and shoulders above all others to make it a safe, sure, and successful investment are the population explosion, leverage and tax shelter. It is interesting to explore each one of these.

Let's look at population. With just a few figures we can get a whole picture of what is happening to real estate. The population of the United States has grown rapidly.

1790	3,929,000
1850	23,261,000
1900	76,094,000
1925	115,832,000
1950	151,683,000
1960	179,232,175
1968	200,827,000
1979	225,000,000

In the first hundred years, we had an increase of about 190 per cent. In the next fifty years we had a 200 per cent increase. In the last eighteen years we had a 140 per cent increase. All those eggheads who deal with projections into the future of things we can't basically put our finger on have come up with an interesting estimate. They say that the population of the United States in 1982 will be 250,000,000. In the year 2000, which is only twenty years away, the population will be 361,000,000. What will that mean to those of us who own real estate?

While we have never lost the fun or formula of making more people, we have no known formula for creating more land. And it gets back to the old thing of supply and demand. As an investor in real estate, what concerns you? Your concern is that, as what you bought becomes scarce, it becomes more valuable. We have more buyers than we have products. This forces the price up. It's almost a sure guarantee that real estate values are going to go up now, five years from now, ten, fifteen, twenty and thirty years from now. This is within the life span of 95 per cent of our readers.

Let's look at the improved pieces of property. Apartment houses that are now up are going to get older. But as a piece of real estate grows older it doesn't become less costly or cheaper. It just doesn't work out that way. The economics of real estate have proved it over so many years. If you have an improved piece of real estate, it is going to appreciate in value providing it is well-kept and the location and economy are stable. We have had a tremendous inflation spiral for many years, and reducing it to under 3 per cent yearly seems impossible. That means we are going to have more income from our present properties. The price of new property is going up and construction costs will increase greatly. New financing will be much higher. Today's property will be worth much, much more in the future. Let's couple this with leverage.

LEVERAGE

Leverage is like a nationwide club. There is no initiation fee, and there are no dues. The only thing necessary to belong to this particular club is to have a case of the *smarts*. It is called the O.P.M. Club.

O.P.M. means Other People's Money. Who are some of the members? Insurance companies have been lifelong members of the O.P.M. Club. They use other people's money constantly. Also, banks, savings and loan associations and other savings institutions are old, old members of the O.P.M. Club. They use our money, your money and other people's money. They are sophisticated investors, and they know how to make other people's money work for them.

All of these charter members use other people's money to invest in real estate. The reason is simple. They can get the greatest possible amount of leverage in the purchase of real estate. Basically, the use of leverage goes like this:

Let's say that a man named Jones buys an apartment house for $100,000 cash. He holds the building for five years, and sells it for $120,000. Jones has a net profit of $20,000 for the five years of ownership. Right?

Well, let's also say that one of the more astute members of the O.P.M. Club bought the same type of apartment house right across the street from Jones. He purchased it for $100,000, but he only put down $20,000. He mortgaged the remaining $80,000. At the end of five years, he found a buyer at $120,000. Did he have a net profit of $20,000? No. He borrowed $80,000 from Other People. Five years later he makes a $20,000 profit on a $20,000 investment of his own. If you figure out the entire transaction you'll see that he gained even more than that. The mortgage was being paid off by his wonderful, wonderful tenants. Actually, he made approximately $12,000 to $15,000 in addition to the $20,000. Now how do you beat that? You don't!

The same thing works on the purchase of land. The reason so many of our forefathers have made so much money on land is that they purchased land in the path of progress. Knowledgeable real estate investment counselors recommended land that looked like it had everything to make a certain success in five, ten or twenty years.

Astute purchasers of land normally put down as little cash as possible. They go for extreme leverage, and any knowledgeable real estate investment counselor can find exceedingly good terms because he knows how to present the entire sales contract to the seller. This grants maximum leverage for the buyer. Fortunes have been made and are *being* made in land because of profit from the use of leverage and the increase in value.

Naturally, not everyone wants to take lots of risk or have

heavy, high mortgages. Fortunately, within the field of real estate, we can just about cut the cloth to suit the client. In other words, you can make an exceedingly conservative purchase, all in cash. You can make a moderate purchase, with 50 per cent cash. And you can make a highly leveraged purchase with the absolute minimum of cash involved. Your knowledgeable real estate investment counselor can tailor this to suit you and your goals. Population explosion coupled with leverage is great, and you can tie these factors with the advantages gained by numerous tax shelters. These are fantastic advantages to owners of real estate.

Never forget that real estate is the only investment wherein we talk of after-tax return on our investment. All other investments bombard us with the per cent return on our investment. It is entirely false to believe that return on your investment is money you can spend. It does not belong to you. Uncle Sam takes his slice of profits. What's left is yours. We call it "Keep Money." There are hardly any investments within those available in the real estate field that don't offer some or many tax shelters. Real estate offers you more "keep money" than any other investment.

Leverage means the intelligent use of banks, insurance companies, pension funds and seller's money. It's mortgaging. Where else can you create a debt on an investment and have someone else pay the debt off for you? Nowhere!

This is the fabulous thing about real estate. We buy an apartment house for $100,000 and we get an $80,000 mortgage. It's written for over fifteen to twenty-five years, payable monthly. Who pays off this debt? Yes, that's right. Those wonderful, wonderful tenants.

Each and every month they strive, struggle, figure, con, sacrifice and scheme on how they can pay the rent. They make deposits to the landlord's account, and he can pay the debts against the building and the expenses. At the end of the term of the mortgage, fifteen or twenty years later, they all get together, and they have a mortgage-burning party. They present you, the owner, with your property free and clear.

They have struggled to pay this off for you. You have gained the advantages of the ownership of real estate, depreciation, tax shelters and the income of the property. When someone had to move and go elsewhere during the twenty years, there was always someone ready and waiting to take over their load of the debt. Someone always wants to come in as a new tenant and assume that part of your obligation. Where else can you find any other investment such as this?

A friend of ours by the name of Stan Harris, who is an exceedingly knowledgeable real estate investment counselor, conducts regular seminars for potential investors. Included in these groups are professional people, doctors, dentists, surgeons, professors, airline pilots, CPA's, clerks, school teachers, truck drivers, book-keepers, etc. On one occasion he invited us to attend one of his meetings. He asked us to talk on investment real estate for five or ten minutes. While talking of the fabulous advantages of mortgaged income property, Stan interrupted with a wave of both his arms. His audience, about seventy-five people, all started to sing in unison. The song came out like this, to the tune of the Notre Dame Fight Song:

> They never stagger
> They never fall
> They pay the rent
> And give us their all
> When we rent a place to them
> It's back to the bank with more
>
> Our fortunes grow
> The mortgage goes down
> They pay the way
> While we go to town
> Wonderful you tenants are
> It's hats off and thanks to you
>
> Oh God bless you tenants all
> We're so glad for crowded halls
> All we say is keep it up
> And we'll love you forever more
> Rah! Rah! Rah!

Stan told us that he begins every seminar like this. He has everyone rise, and they all sing with gusto. A great idea.

PLANNED MILLIONAIREHOOD

"Ninety per cent of all millionaires become so through owning real estate. More money has been made in real estate than in all industrial investments combined. The wise young man or wage earner of today invests his money in real estate."—Andrew Carnegie

In Dallas, Texas, there lives a widow. Let's call her "Betty Smith." When her husband died, she was forty-one. She set out deliberately to become a millionaire. She gave herself a calendar of twenty years to succeed.

Her husband had only had a small cash value life insurance policy of $8,000 and it hardly gave her enough money to live. She knew that she had to do something other than just trying to get an odd job. So, after a lot of investigating within the field of investments, she chose real estate. It was something she could devote her time to, and it was something that seemed safe and sound. She threw herself into it.

She acquired a total of eight single-family homes she was using as rental units. One day she realized that the repairs, upkeep and expenses of holding these eight different homes were eating up her expected profit. All she was gaining was the payoff of the mortgages by her tenants. She finally realized that if she would combine these eight units, and exchange them for one large apartment house, she would greatly reduce the expenses, headaches and heartaches.

She used her equity in these homes as a down payment on a twelve-unit apartment house. At the same time, she received some invaluable advice from a real estate investment counselor. He told her, "Use as little cash of your own as possible. Use other people's money, and get as much mortgage as you can safely handle. It doesn't matter if you have to pay a few more dollars a month, as long as the property is self-liquidating."

She realized that her cost of management would be no more for a large place. So she traded the apartment house in as a down payment on a thirty-unit apartment house. Eventually, she traded her equity in this apartment house, plus a few thousand dollars cash, for a down payment on a sixty-unit apartment house. While she was doing this, she relied on an old axiom of real estate, which spells out the three prime requisites of a good investment—location, location, location.

Her primary objective was not to see how much cash flow she could get out of these buildings, but to see how rapidly she could build up equities within the buildings. She could climb higher and faster by acquiring larger properties. She usually looked for buildings that were a little run down, but in excellent locations. With imagination and some refinancing capital, she would cure the problem of the building and put it back on at a high rental.

She has purchased each property with one thought in mind, and that was the possibility of selling it. Mrs. Smith is more than halfway to her goal. While she is sleeping, her tenants are concerning themselves about paying off her mortgages, and she's practicing planned millionairehood.

CHAPTER 14

HOW TO GET STARTED IN REAL ESTATE

By now you probably like what you've read about the wild possibilities in real estate. It could be, too, that you're saying, "Ah, great, but it's for the guys with a whole lot of money. Yeah, you've gotta have money to be a winner in the real estate business . . . just like everything else."

And maybe you're the kind who says, "Sure, I'd go all the way in real estate, but I don't want to endanger my savings. What the heck, I've been saving that all of my life. I sure don't want to take any chances with a bunch of slickers in the real estate business."

Or, it could be that you're saying, "These guys aren't serious. It sounds too easy. Why, if it was that easy to get rich, then how come everybody ain't doin' it?"

You don't have to do anything. You don't have to invest in real estate or anything else if you don't want to. That's the easy way to poverty, however. And it doesn't matter too much to us if you want to be in that other 95 per cent. It makes the competition a little easier on the rest of us when you don't give a damn about your own future. But one of these days you'll be there. You'll be at a point in life when you have to ask yourself a bunch of real important questions. You'll have to tell yourself just how much you've been able to accomplish in this short life of ours. And, in case you haven't thought about it, we're here for the quickest blink in time.

A scientist friend of ours gave us this example of just how relative we are to time.

He said that if the height of the Empire State Building represented the age of the earth, you could put a quarter on the sidewalk next to it, and that thickness would represent how long man has been on this earth.

Now, it seems to us that, if you try to take seventy-year slices out of that quarter's thickness, then you can hardly see that you've been here at all. Yet everything we do has to take place in that little slice, and that's cutting things real thin.

You have to do something between your birthday and your

death day to let yourself notice that you've been here, too. It's your life, and you can live it with as much success as you want. But you're the one person in time . . . a long, long time . . . who has any chance at all to do anything at all about your life. You get just one chance. You can't say, "Oops," because you don't get to try again. You get one try, that's all.

We feel that success comes in many forms for everyone. People who are happy are successful. They are happy about what they have done. Every time you set a little goal, and then reach it, you are able to enjoy success. If your goals are money and riches, then go after them. If your goals are comfort and happiness for your family, then go after those. But how about combining the two? Now that's not such a bad idea. No one is really going to be made at you if you become rich. They might be a little green around the gills with envy, but that's not a real serious case of being mad.

If having a little money makes you happy, then why deprive yourself of that simple reward for being a little sharper than the next guy . . . or 95 per cent of the next guys?

"Okay, okay," you plead. "We agree," you shout. "You're so smart. We like what you're saying—but how do we get started?"

You've read the book. You *have* started. Maybe it's your first step, but that's always the important one. There's an old German saying, which we can't spell, but it translates to this: All beginnings are difficult.

This goes for cutting your grass, jogging to health, going to school, and everything you can think of. But you have to get the lawn mower out of the garage, or you have to get used to the dogs chasing you and the fat guys honking at you as you sweat your rear end off before you've jogged from the corner to the alley. You have to start. And you can't say, "Gee if I'd only taken a crack at it, just think where I'd be." It's seldom too late to start. You may never catch up, but at least you'll be on your way.

Therefore, we'd like to congratulate you on getting off your dead parts to make a start. Just reading this book has given you a start toward a greater success. We don't propose, in any way, that what you've read here will make you a success. You have to do that. If you blow it, which probably won't happen, you can't call us up and chew on us because you didn't make it. If you do, we'll probably just say that you didn't try hard enough. We know, for sure, that if you try, something good will happen to you. If you want to get on the happy wagon with real estate, then you have to make the first move. That spells effort. And effort spells success.

If you want to know more about anything we've discussed in

the book, look into the many possible sources of information. Go to your library. Get the current best-selling, exotic sex thriller if you want, but pick up a copy of a book on real estate at the same time. Such books offer a degree of pleasure and excitement, too. You can identify with success in real estate because it's so possible for you to be there.

Seek out a knowledgeable real estate investment counselor. You can't learn about the stock market just by reading the financial pages. You have to listen to people who are in the business. You have to learn from people who can teach you something. This is true in real estate, too.

Investing in real estate today is more complicated than it was just a few years ago. The underlying question each investor must answer is, "What is happening in the economy today?" If conditions seem to indicate a forthcoming recession, investing now and using a great deal of leverage would be a mistake. Contrary to this, if inflation is what appears to be continuing, buy now and leverage everything as much as is available. Only you, the investor, can decide this.

There is one particular investment philosophy that seems to work under nearly any condition. We call it the belt and suspender operation. That is, the investor who has decided to make his property produce money, no matter what. He jumps into the situation with both feet—doing necessary repairs himself. He cuts every corner possible. He does everything wise to increase income. He will probably survive any economic downturn.

The other type of investor who leaves the day-to-day operation to just anyone, goes about his own business, and leaves his property to take second fiddle may see tough times ahead.

Now, consider this: the most profitable dollars you may ever spend in real estate investing may be a truly professional consultant. He can stand outside your situation and evaluate things as they really are. Don't be afraid to spend the money—getting started right and making periodic checkups on your progress can make you big money. Just be careful to select the right person to be your adviser.

When you find such a man, be frank and honest with him. He'll do the same for you. The first stage of his counseling service to you will involve a meaningful study of where you are and where you want to go. He'll want to know your long- and short-term goals.

Your first meeting with him will take a couple of hours. It takes some time for the two of you to get to know each other, and it'll take some time for you to paint a true picture of your financial position for him. It'll take some time for him to tell you about his company . . . a company which will be backing him and you in the years to come.

If the man you see says, "I've got just the thing for you," ten minutes after you've been there, forget it. He doesn't. All he wants to do is peddle property.

The right kind of guy for you says, "I'm not real sure at this point if you should even think about investing in real estate. Let's find out." Yeah, he's the pro. He's the guy who will go to the trouble of finding out if real estate really is the thing for you or not. After he has completed his investigation, he's the kind of a guy who'll tell you if it is or if it isn't.

We know of cases like that. Some people aren't ready to invest in anything because they don't have enough money, which doesn't have to be much, or they don't know what they want in the future.

You'll agree. You need some money to invest in anything. How much depends on what you want to do. If you do have a little money to invest, then see if you have any goals. What do you want out of life that will be possible if you make some wise investments? If you never invest (gasp!), you should at least have some goals.

The investment counselor will want some information from your attorney and from your accountant. He's nosy, but he has to be if he's going to be able to make a sound recommendation. If he's sharp, that's all he'll do at that point. He'll just recommend. Then he'll test your desires. He'll see if you want to be a champ in the other 5 per cent.

It is up to you. People have the decision of success. You must decide on your future and the future of your family. The real estate investment counselor can't make the decision. It isn't his job, and he can't walk around in your skin.

We've tried to point out the advantages of real estate. We feel that they are fantastic, and we wish you'd join us on the trip to the other 5 per cent party. It's a gas, and we're not about to miss one minute of it. Real estate, to us, is *the* way to get there.

To us, real estate is the ideal investment. But we won't go that far with you. You have to decide on your own investments. There isn't one single, ideal investment for anyone. In the most successful cases, ideal investments are combinations of investments.

But look at real estate from this angle. Where else can you make a small down payment on a piece of income-producing property that will be paid off in twenty years—while during this time your wonderful, wonderful tenants break their backs to make the monthly rent?

In twenty years they bring the mortgage to you, and with pride they say, "Here you are. We finally paid it off for you."

You didn't pay for it. It cost you $10,000 down. The original price was $50,000. During the twenty years it appreciated to $75,000. What did it cost you? Just the $10,000, friend. And who paid for it? Your buddies, the tenants.

There is only one thing you can do to insure your absolute failure in life. That's inaction. If you don't do something, how are you going to make any progress? The poor 95 per cent can demonstrate the results of not doing anything but saving their money and buying insurance for the future.

Real estate pays, and it can pay big. It's the kind of thing that fits into life's trio of activities. It can fit into your life without any disruption of your life. And it can make your life much sweeter.

To some of us, real estate is the work-and-play part of life. To others it's all play. But those of us who are successful in real estate have an edge on the rest of the world. We even have fun with real estate while sleeping. It is the only way we know of having something really working for you when you aren't doing a damn thing but having sweet dreams.

Real estate investing is how to get rich while you sleep.

"Real estate is an imperishable asset, ever increasing in value; it is the most solid security that human ingenuity has devised. It is the basis of all security and about the only indestructible security."   ——Russell Sage